Case Studies of Existing

Human Tissue Repositories

"Best Practices" for a Biospecimen Resource for the Genomic and Proteomic Era

Elisa Eiseman

Gabrielle Bloom

Jennifer Brower

Noreen Clancy

Stuart S. Olmsted

Prepared for the National Cancer Institute
and the National Dialogue on Cancer

 SCIENCE AND TECHNOLOGY

The research described in this report was conducted by RAND Science and Technology for the National Cancer Institute and National Dialogue on Cancer.

Library of Congress Cataloging-in-Publication Data

Case studies of existing human tissue repositories : "best practices" for a biospecimen resource for the genomic and proteomic era / Elisa Eiseman ... [et al.].
    p. cm.
    "MG-120."
    Includes bibliographical references.
    ISBN 0-8330-3527-4 (pbk.)
    1. Tissue banks—case studies. 2. Preservation of organs, tissues, etc.—Case studies. 3. Cadaver homografts—Case studies.
    [DNLM: 1. Tissue Banks—standards—United States. 2. Organizational Case Studies—United States. 3. Tissue Preservation—methods—United States. QS 523 C337 2004] I. Eiseman, Elisa. II. Rand Corporation.

RD127.C375 2004
362.17'83—dc22

2003024742

The RAND Corporation is a nonprofit research organization providing objective analysis and effective solutions that address the challenges facing the public and private sectors around the world. RAND's publications do not necessarily reflect the opinions of its research clients and sponsors.

RAND® is a registered trademark.

Cover design by Peter Soriano

Published 2003 by the RAND Corporation
1700 Main Street, P.O. Box 2138, Santa Monica, CA 90407-2138
1200 South Hayes Street, Arlington, VA 22202-5050
201 North Craig Street, Suite 202, Pittsburgh, PA 15213-1516
RAND URL: http://www.rand.org/
To order RAND documents or to obtain additional information, contact
Distribution Services: Telephone: (310) 451-7002;
Fax: (310) 451-6915; Email: order@rand.org

Preface

Human tissue has been collected and stored at institutions in the United States for more than 100 years. Each of these institutions, or repositories, was established to meet a specific set of objectives, and its design is integrally linked to those objectives. Tissue collection, processing, and storage techniques vary depending on the purpose of the repository, as do the quality and extent of information collected with the biospecimens.

Over the last year, the National Biospecimen Network (NBN) Design Team, a subset of the Tissue Access Working Group (TAWG) convened by the National Dialogue on Cancer (NDC) to address "access to appropriately collected, consented, and annotated tissue," has been drafting a blueprint for a national biospecimen network. The overall goal of the TAWG is

> to establish a national, pre-competitive, regulatory compliant and genetic-privacy protected, standardized, inclusive, highest quality network of biological sample(s) banks; developed in partnerships with and supported by cancer survivors/advocates; shared, readily accessible, and searchable using appropriate informatics systems (e.g., amenable to molecular profiling capability).

To assist in its examination of existing tissue resources, the NBN Design Team requested that the RAND Corporation conduct case studies of existing human tissue resources to evaluate their utility for genomics- and proteomics-based cancer research and that RAND identify "best practices" at these institutions. This report presents the

RAND findings for each repository evaluated and identifies best practices that can be used by the TAWG in its strategic planning process for the development of a new NBN.

About RAND Science and Technology

RAND Science and Technology (RAND S&T), a unit of the RAND Corporation, conducts research and analysis that helps government and corporate decisionmakers address opportunities and challenges created by scientific innovation and rapid technological change. RAND S&T's work stretches from emerging energy technologies to global environmental change to still other endeavors seeking a better understanding of the nation's scientific enterprise and how best to nurture it. Focal points of RAND S&T work include energy, the environment, information technology, aerospace issues, technology and economic development, bioethics, advanced materials, and "critical" technologies for industries and occupations.

RAND S&T serves a variety of clients, including federal, state, and local government agencies, foreign governments, foundations, and private organizations. The S&T team has a wide range of expertise and includes physicists and geophysicists; chemists and geochemists; electrical, chemical, mechanical, and information technology engineers; biological and environmental scientists; and economists and other social scientists.

Inquiries regarding RAND Science and Technology may be directed to:

Stephen Rattien
Director, RAND Science and Technology
The RAND Corporation
1200 South Hayes Street
Arlington, VA 22202-5050
Phone: (703) 413-1100 x5219
Email: contact-st@rand.org
Website: www.rand.org/scitech/

The RAND Corporation Quality Assurance Process

Every RAND publication, database, and major briefing is carefully peer reviewed before its release. For more than 50 years, decision-makers in the public and private sectors have turned to RAND for objective analysis and effective solutions that address the challenges facing the nation and the world. In carrying out its work on behalf of clients and the larger public, RAND confronts different analytical challenges over time. However, its principles remain constant. RAND research and analysis aims to

- provide practical guidance by making choices clear and addressing barriers to effective implementation of policies and decisions
- develop innovative solutions to complex problems by bringing together researchers in all relevant academic specialties
- achieve objectivity by avoiding partisanship and vested interests
- meet the highest technical standards by employing advanced empirical methods and rigorous peer review
- serve the public interest by wide dissemination of its publications.

RAND also conducts periodic external and internal reviews of the quality of its body of work. For additional details regarding the RAND Corporation Quality Assurance Program, visit

http://www.rand.org/about/standards/

Contents

CHAPTER FOUR

CHAPTER FIVE

CHAPTER SIX

Figure and Tables

Figure

Tables

Summary

The National Dialogue on Cancer

The National Dialogue on Cancer (NDC) is a forum that brings together representatives from the private sector, academia, non-profit organizations, and government agencies to accelerate progress against cancer. At a March 2002 meeting of the NDC Research Team, "access to appropriately collected, consented, and annotated tissue" was identified as a critical barrier to developing genomics- and proteomics-based therapies. Following this meeting, the Tissue Access Working Group (TAWG) was formed to address this barrier.

The TAWG first met in August 2002 and concluded that the development of a national tissue resource and data bank was necessary if the nation was to ultimately realize the promise of genomics and proteomics for preventing and curing cancer as well as a range of other diseases. The overall goal of the TAWG is

> to establish a national, pre-competitive, regulatory compliant and genetic-privacy protected, standardized, inclusive, highest quality network of biological sample(s) banks; developed in partnerships with and supported by cancer survivors/advocates; shared, readily accessible, and searchable using appropriate informatics systems (e.g., amenable to molecular profiling capability).

Over the last year, a subset of the TAWG, the National Biospecimen Network (NBN) Design Team, has been drafting a strategic plan—the NBN Design and Engineering Blueprint—that identifies the key goals and characteristics of a new NBN. In conjunction with its development of the blueprint, the NBN Design Team recognized that it was important to evaluate existing tissue resources. To assist in its examination of existing tissue resources, the team requested that RAND conduct case studies of existing human tissue resources to evaluate their utility for genomics- and proteomics-based cancer research and that RAND identify "best practices" at these institutions.

This report presents the findings for twelve repositories in the United States that represent a broad spectrum of repository types. Interviews were conducted at each repository with key individuals who were asked questions about repository design; the bioinformatics system; privacy, ethical, and legal issues; and public relations and marketing. The interviews focused on the identification of best practices, including innovative strategies, systems and processes pertaining to specimen and data collection, storage and distribution, bioinformatics systems, and informed consent. This report identifies best practices that can be used by the TAWG in its strategic planning process for the development of a robust resource for genomics- and proteomics-based research that will fulfill the needs of the research community.

Evaluation of Existing Human Tissue Resources

Each of the repositories evaluated for this study was established and designed to meet specific objectives. Thus, each repository's design is integrally linked to its objectives. Biospecimen collection, processing, and storage techniques vary depending on the purpose of the repository. Likewise, the quality and extent of information collected with the specimens vary depending on the purpose for which the tissue was originally collected. The type of informed consent—whether general surgical consent or specific informed consent for the use of the biospecimen for research purposes—also varies from repository to repository, sometimes limiting the usefulness of some specimens for certain kinds of research.

While all repositories evaluated for this study have one or more of the features identified by the NBN Design Team as components of a new NBN, none has all of the characteristics identified as necessary for a successful NBN. Some repositories have several of the needed characteristics; others have only a few.

Complicating matters is the fact that there are currently no national standards for tissue repositories that collect and store specimens for research use.[1] Therefore, the way one repository collects, processes, and stores its specimens may be very different from the way another repository does, which may complicate comparisons of research results obtained using biospecimens from different repositories. Furthermore, once samples are distributed to researchers, most repositories do not require those researchers to report their research results back to the repository, and even fewer repositories enter those research results into their bioinformatics systems and make them available to the broader research community.

The NBN Design Team recognized the limitations of existing repositories and decided to design a new kind of repository. The team envisions a network of geographically dispersed tissue repositories to collect, process, store, and distribute appropriately consented diseased and normal tissue and other biological specimens with associated clinical data supported and coordinated by an accessible, user-friendly bioinformatics system networked across the country. The biospecimens would be collected, processed, annotated, stored, and distrib-

---

[1] Professional societies, such as the International Society for Biological and Environmental Repositories (ISBER) and the National Committee for Clinical Laboratory Standards (NCCLS), have recognized the need for standardization and are developing guidance for establishing and operating biospecimen repositories. ISBER is creating a set of Best Practices for Repositories to provide repository professionals with guidance on repository activities. The NCCLS guidelines will cover all health care institutions and clinics that collect human tissue for research purposes, and will provide standards for addressing all issues associated with the collection of human tissue to support biomedical research, including the ethical, legislative, and legal concerns.

uted in a highly standardized manner to minimize experimental variability and accelerate scientific progress. The NBN would also archive research data submitted by investigators who were using NBN samples and would promote data sharing and meta-analysis.

The network of geographically dispersed tissue repositories that the NBN Design Team envisions for collecting, processing, annotating, storing, and distributing tissue is very similar to how some of the repositories evaluated for this study are set up. The Cooperative Human Tissue Network (CHTN), the Early Detection Research Network (EDRN), the Breast and Ovarian Cancer Family Registries (CFRs) (of which the Philadelphia Familial Breast Cancer Registry is a member), and the University of Pittsburgh Health Sciences Tissue Bank (HSTB) are all variations of the model of decentralized resources deployed through a virtual network of geographically dispersed tissue centers coordinated and supported by a centralized bioinformatics and data management system networked across the country. The National Heart, Lung, and Blood Institute (NHLBI) Biological Specimen Repository, the Armed Forces Institute of Pathology (AFIP) National Pathology Repository, Ardais Corporation, and Genomics Collaborative, Inc. (GCI) have a decentralized collection model but maintain their storage and distribution of specimens and their bioinformatics system at one physical location. The Tissue Array Research Program (TARP) also has a decentralized collection model with the bioinformatics system and storage maintained at one physical location; however, its tissue microarrays are distributed by the CHTN. In contrast, the Duke University Breast Specialized Program of Research Excellence (SPORE), the Mayo Clinic Prostate SPORE, and the University of Alabama at Birmingham (UAB) Breast and Ovarian SPOREs have centralized collection, storage, distribution, and bioinformatics systems and data management. Based on its evaluation of these twelve existing human tissue resources, RAND came up with several best practices that the NBN Design Team and NDC may want to consider as they implement their plan for the NBN.

Biospecimen Collection, Processing, Annotation, Storage, and Distribution: Best Practices

Best practices for biospecimen collection that will increase the quantity and variety of high-quality samples available to researchers, while maintaining appropriate normal controls, include establishing a network of collection sites at academic medical centers and community hospitals, and collecting tissues from a broad range of diseases, non-diseased matching adjacent tissue, normal tissue, and other biological specimens (e.g., whole blood, serum, and plasma). It is also important that tissue be collected from ethnically diverse populations of all ages to ensure that the tissue available for research purposes is diverse and demographically representative of the population, and to expand biomedical research to include understudied/underrepresented populations and the study of health disparities.

The prioritization of patient diagnosis over collection of specimens for research purposes is key to ensuring that patient care is not compromised and that patients continue to donate biospecimens. Pathologists at the collection site play an important role in the initial procurement of the specimen for the repository, and repository pathologists are central to the quality control procedures for verification and evaluation of the specimen. In addition, repository-trained personnel using standard operating procedures and standard collection and processing equipment are important to promoting standardized tissue collection and processing.

Best practices for data collection depend on the mission of the repository. However, no matter what the requirements for the amount of associated data are, certain best practices are applicable. It is important to collect consistent and high-quality data associated with biospecimens and to employ a standardized set of common data elements that are collected with every biospecimen. It is also important to define the data set that is optimal for fulfilling the mission of the repository and the needs of its customers, and to collect the data (such as demographic and pathologic data, family history, medical history, lifestyle and diet history, treatment history, and clinical outcomes) required to meet those needs.

Once data are collected, they must be entered into the repository's bioinformatics system. The use of common data elements and standardized terminology for data collection procedures allows the use of standardized data-entry forms with features that minimize the errors introduced while typing information into forms. In addition, scannable bar codes are used to track biospecimens and associated information throughout their lifetime at the repository. Parsing techniques are used to flag discrepancies and to record errors and their reconciliation. The use of standardized terminology and computer data entry forms, scannable bar codes, and data reconciliation techniques are best practices that ensure data accuracy.

Standards for storage depend on tissue type and preservation condition (e.g., snap frozen, paraffin embedded, tissue microarray). Snap-frozen specimens are commonly stored at −80°C in mechanical freezers or in liquid nitrogen. Paraffin-embedded tissue and tissue microarrays are stored at room temperature or in a climate-controlled environment to protect them from melting or other damage. However, there is no consensus on the optimum storage conditions for specimens.

Once specimens are placed in storage, it is necessary to monitor storage conditions and maintain equipment. Standard operating procedures for freezer maintenance, adequate backup equipment, and redundancy in storage location are best practices for ensuring that specimens are stored and maintained at the necessary temperature and condition and that specimen integrity is not compromised. Periodic auditing, inventories, and certification of the location, identity, and quality of specimens ensure the quality and integrity of samples sent to researchers. Bar coded inventory systems are used to track specimen storage location.

Standardized and carefully monitored shipping procedures track all shipments in and out of a repository. Biospecimens sent to a repository from remote/satellite collection sites and samples sent from that repository to researchers are tracked using electronic technologies, such as bar coded inventory systems or smart chips and radio-frequency identification tags.

Specimen distribution practices clearly depend on the mission of the repository. If the mission is to provide tissue samples to as broad a base of researchers as possible based on the quality of the proposed research, then biospecimen distribution policies should be established to fulfill this mission. If the mission is clearly defined, and if the repository evaluates its ability to meet its goals and changes its policies, procedures, and practices when not meeting those goals, then this is a best practice.

Quality assurance is fundamental to the successful operation of any biospecimen repository. The use of standardized protocols for collection, storage, processing, and distribution of specimens, and the use of common data elements for the annotation of specimens at each of the individual network participant locations make comparative research across participating institutions possible. To ensure that the collection, processing, annotation, storage, and distribution of biospecimens occur at a consistently high level of quality, it is necessary to have a multitiered, fully integrated quality assurance system and standard operating procedures. Quality assurance starts with the training of personnel before biospecimens are ever collected and includes everything up through considering researcher feedback on sample quality.

Bioinformatics: Best Practices

The backbone of any repository is a standardized, scalable, and secure bioinformatics system that is appropriate for repository management, tissue acquisition and management, and data aggregation and analysis. Bioinformatics systems are used for repository management, clinical and pathological data management, collection and analysis of research results, and data mining and advanced statistical analysis to identify patterns and establish relationships. A bioinformatics system that is searchable and minable via varying levels of Web-based access for different individuals—including repository personnel, researchers, patients, and the public—is a best practice. Robust network security systems and access control are crucial to ensure that the privacy of the tissue source is protected and that the bioinformatics system is secure.

Bioinformatics systems can range from simple databases to proprietary systems developed in house. Close ties between bioinformatics system developers, researchers, data managers, and repository management allow the bioinformatics system to be designed so that it is responsive to the needs of multiple user types.

The use of a standardized language to categorize and describe biospecimens and enter data into the bioinformatics system is essential for comparison of biospecimen characteristics among collection sites. In addition to using a standardized language, it is also important to use either a system that can automatically extract data from medical records or multiple checks of data entry to ensure the accuracy of the data in the bioinformatics system.

Consumer/User Needs: Best Practices

A repository is successful only if it is meeting user needs, and its success can only be determined through continual self-assessment and re-evaluation. Meeting user needs may require different approaches depending on the repository's design, customer profile, and product offerings. Assessing the needs of researchers, tracking the numbers and types of tissue samples distributed, and using this information to determine whether the resource is continuing to meet researchers' needs or whether changes need to be made constitute a best practice.

The review and prioritization system for tissue distribution generally falls into one of four general categories: (1) first come, first served; (2) priority to members of the network, collaborators, and/or contributors to the repository; (3) prioritization based on merit review of research proposals; or (4) prioritization based on a set policy of the repository. Best practices to ensure equitable distribution of tissue to the broadest group of researchers possible include (a) the use of a tissue utilization committee to prioritize tissue distribution based on merit review of researcher proposals, and (b) policies to control the distribution of rare specimens, to control the last sample of a particular specimen, and to prevent the control of an entire specimen or type of specimen by one researcher. Giving priority to researchers at collecting institutions is also a best practice, one that leads to more support for the resource and higher investment in the quality of the specimens collected.

Committees or review groups in which both providers and consumers are able to provide input on the usefulness of the repository resources are valuable in evaluating how well the repository meets user needs. In addition, solicitation of feedback on sample quality directly from researchers who are using the samples helps to identify systemic problems, inconsistencies, or problems with the specimens in the repository or specimens being collected in a certain way or from a certain collection site. These best practices enable repositories to improve specimen quality and to be responsive to researcher needs.

Business Plan and Operations: Best Practices

Repositories are generally funded by four different sources: the federal government, academia, private industry, and private non-profit. Repositories also follow different business models, including tissue banking versus prospective collection and distribution, networks versus individual sites, and centralized versus decentralized collection, storage, and bioinformatics systems. Establishing a network of collection sites at academic medical centers and community hospitals to perform a combination of banking to collect and maintain a ready supply of tissue and prospective collection to meet researcher needs is a best practice.

When approaching a medical facility about becoming a participating collection site, it is often more productive to start discussions with the pathologists and surgeons rather than with hospital administrators. Once a relationship has been established at a collection site, it is vital to maintain close working relationships with surgeons, pathologists, nurses, and other relevant staff at that site through good communication between the repository and collection site.

At the repositories evaluated, the cost per specimen to collect, process, store, and distribute was variable (between $60 and $150 per specimen at the repositories able to provide estimates) and depended on the amount of clinical information accompanying the biospecimen—the more information, the higher the cost of collecting the tissue and associated data. The cost of samples to researchers ranged from free of charge to $200 or higher depending on the type of sample obtained, the level of annotation associated with the sample, and whether the researcher was from an academic institution or industry. Accurately determining the actual costs of collecting, processing, storing, and distributing tissue samples, and operating on a cost recovery basis to financially sustain the repository constitute a best practice.

Continually assessing new technologies and taking measures to develop and incorporate new technologies into the repository are necessary for any system to be forward thinking, capable of expansion, and flexible as researchers' needs change. This is usually accomplished through regular meetings with staff to brainstorm about ways to address and incorporate new technologies, in combination with more formal mechanisms, such as committees or workshops established to purposefully scan for improvements and new technologies. Requiring acknowledgment in publications for the use of repository resources, including specific language for such acknowledgment, is a best practice because it raises the visibility of the resource and may encourage future donations and use of the resource. It also allows the tracking of scientific accomplishments made possible by the availability of specimens from the resource.

Privacy, Ethical Concerns, and Consent Issues: Best Practices

Institutional review boards (IRBs) are responsible for the oversight and review of research that involves human participants to ensure that their privacy is protected and confidentiality of data is maintained. Requiring repositories to have IRB approval for the collection, storage, and distribution of biospecimens and associated data, and requiring researchers requesting samples to have IRB approval of research projects that will use the samples are essential for protecting privacy and confidentiality. In addition, convening a bioethics advisory board or other governance and oversight board/committee to oversee privacy and confidentiality procedures provides another layer of review. Limiting access to the codes that link patient identifying information to the sources of the tissue specimens through physical and/or cyber procedures to minimize the chance of identifying information being released is also a best practice to protect privacy and confidentiality.

Obtaining biospecimens from individuals who are fully informed about and have consented to the collection of their tissue by the repository and its use for research purposes is a best practice. Using a tiered consent process that allows individuals to choose the type of specimen(s), if any, they want to donate (e.g., tissue, blood, or urine), the type of research the specimen can be used for (e.g., a specific research project, general research, or genetic research), and whether their medical records and outcomes data can be accessed is also a best practice. Ideally, the consent process should occur separately from the surgical consent. However, since this is not always possible, at a minimum the informed consent for the collection and research use of specimens should be a separate section of the surgical consent form that requires a separate signature.

Intellectual Property and Legal Issues: Best Practices

Individuals who contribute biospecimens must have the right to withdraw their consent and have their tissue removed from the repository. However, once the tissue has been stripped of identifiers so that the link back to the identity of the tissue source has been destroyed, it is not possible to identify the tissue to withdraw it from the repository. Beyond the right to withdraw their consent and their tissue from the repository, tissue sources are given no other rights to their tissues by most repositories. It is a best practice to allow an individual who contributes tissue to a repository to withdraw consent and have the tissue, data, and computer records removed from the repository if the tissue retains identifiers to link it to that individual and it has not been distributed to researchers.

Most repositories do not retain downstream rights to any intellectual property produced through the use of the tissues they distribute. In most cases, institutions that contribute biospecimens to the repository give up their rights to the biospecimens as well. However, some contributing institutions are given priority for tissue requests. In the interest of being clear and to avoid conflicts with tissue sources, researchers using the tissue, or institutions contributing biospecimens, it is a best practice to use a specific published policy on intellectual property. Another best practice is to prioritize tissue distribution based on need while reserving a small percentage of tissue for contributing institutions participating in the repository.

Requiring researchers to sign an agreement that covers the legal issues associated with the use of biospecimens is a best practice. The tissue use agreement should contain language to the effect that the specimens will be used only for the purposes cited in the application, no attempt to obtain identifying information will be made, no specimens will be sold or shared with a third party without the prior written permission of the repository, all specimens will be treated as potentially infectious, all personnel who will be handling the specimens will be properly trained, there is no implied warranty on the specimens, any publications resulting from the use of repository specimens will acknowledge the repository, and the researcher/institution using the tissue assumes responsibility for all risks associated with the receipt, handling, storage, and use of the tissue.

The matter of liability with respect to safety issues associated with the use of the specimens, loss of privacy or breach of confidentiality of tissue sources, claims by tissue sources of physical/ psychosocial harms, or claims of tissue sources to property rights for discoveries made using their tissues is a major concern to repositories. Therefore, it is important to explicitly specify the responsibility for assuming risks in connection with use of biospecimens, to fully inform tissue sources about risks to their rights and welfare, and to clarify ownership issues in tissue use agreements and during the informed consent process. Similarly, it is a best practice to carefully review researchers' submissions and credentials to ensure that tissue is being used by legitimate researchers for legitimate purposes. This review should include the inspection of IRB documentation, review of the study design for which the samples will be used, and verification that the researcher requesting samples is associated with a legitimate research institution.

Public Relations, Marketing, and Education: Best Practices

Public relations, marketing, and education are critical to the success of any tissue repository. Utilizing a combination of approaches to publicize the resources available at the repository—including exhibits at scientific meetings, advertising in scientific journals, newsletters, Web sites, direct mailings, and word of mouth—is a successful way to increase the visibility of the repository, its resources, and its mission. Although not widely done today, a best practice for repositories is to provide feedback to tissue sources, physicians, and researchers through scientific and patient workshops that report generalized research findings, by disseminating research news and patient education information on a Web site, by sending newsletters to tissue sources and researchers summarizing research with repository resources, or through other outreach venues.

Conclusions

Each of the repositories evaluated in this study was designed according to a specific vision, which was not necessarily the same as the vision of the NBN Design Team. Due to these different visions, none of the repositories in this report exhibits *all* of the elements identified as important by the NBN Design Team for the proposed NBN. However, in most cases the repositories are flexible and, with appropriate funding and guidelines, have the potential to be an integral part of the NBN. In fact, this study revealed that most of the repositories have undergone a significant learning curve and that their current successes are based on years of experience and learning from early operations. This wealth of experience should not be overlooked as NDC goes forward with its plan to establish a new NBN.

All of the repositories evaluated exhibit some characteristics that would be useful for an NBN, but some of the repositories incorporate more of the NBN Design Team requirements than others do. CHTN, University of Pittsburgh HSTB, Ardais, and GCI have several of the characteristics identified by the NBN Design Team as necessary for a successful NBN. CHTN is a virtual network with the proven ability to distribute tens of thousands of biospecimens in a variety of forms (e.g., fresh, snap frozen, and paraffin embedded) to meet researchers' needs. University of Pittsburgh HSTB has developed a Web-based bioinformatics system that includes proteomics and genomics information and is already being used in Pennsylvania to create a virtual network of repositories. Ardais and GCI, the two private companies in this study, have streamlined specimen collection, processing, storage, and distribution through specific standard operating procedures, and they both minimize operator and data entry errors through the use of bar-code systems.

Other repositories only have a few of the key components of the proposed NBN. For example, TARP develops and disseminates tissue microarrays for high-throughput screening of multiple tumor tissues (300 to 500 tissues per array). EDRN requires that specimens be collected, processed, and annotated in a standardized manner and that a set of common data elements be collected with each specimen. Philadelphia Familial Breast Cancer Registry also uses common data elements, and it routinely collects longitudinal data. The SPOREs at Duke University, the Mayo Clinic, and UAB routinely collect detailed clinical information and longitudinal data.

Whether NDC decides to fulfill the NBN goal by building a brand new repository or by using existing repositories in the development of a national network, learning from the existing repositories will be an important step. This report identifies the best practices at twelve biospecimen repositories in the United States. As the NBN gets under way, more detailed analyses of existing biospecimen repositories and the inclusion of key personnel from existing repositories will be warranted.

Acknowledgments

The principal investigator, Elisa Eiseman, would like to acknowledge that Gabrielle Bloom, Jennifer Brower, Noreen Clancy, and Stuart S. Olmsted all contributed equally to this report. This report was truly a team effort, so their names appear alphabetically and not in order of level of effort.

The authors would like to thank all of the repository personnel who were enthusiastic and cooperative participants in the interviews and provided invaluable information about the operations and best practices at their repositories:

Cooperative Human Tissue Network (CHTN):
- Roger Aamodt, Ph.D., Chief, Resources Development Branch, Cancer Diagnosis Program, Division of Cancer Treatment and Diagnosis (DCTD), National Cancer Institute (NCI), National Institutes of Health (NIH)
- Marianna Bledsoe, Program Director, Resources Development Branch, Cancer Diagnosis Program, DCTD, NCI, NIH

CHTN Eastern Division, University of Pennsylvania:
- Virginia LiVolsi, M.D., Principal Investigator
- Kelly Feil, Director
- Dee McGarvey, Manager

Tissue Array Research Program (TARP):
- Stephen M. Hewitt, M.D., Ph.D., Director of TARP, NCI

Early Detection Research Network (EDRN):
- Sudhir Srivastava, Ph.D., M.P.H., Program Director, EDRN Coordination Office
- Donald Johnsey, EDRN Information Technology Manager

Philadelphia Familial Breast Cancer Registry/Breast and Ovarian Cancer Family Registries:
- Mary Daly, M.D., Ph.D., Principal Investigator, Philadelphia Familial Breast Cancer Registry at the Fox Chase Cancer Center
- Jeanne Beck, Ph.D., Professor, Coriell Institute for Medical Research; Director, Coriell Cell Repositories (CCR)

National Heart, Lung, and Blood Institute Biological Specimen Repository:
- Kathi Shea, Director, Repository Operations, BBI Biotech
- Susan Sherer, Senior Study Coordinator, Lymphangioleiomyomatosis (LAM) Registry Data Coordinating Center, Cleveland Clinic

Armed Forces Institute of Pathology (AFIP) National Pathology Repository:
- Francis Gannon, M.D., Chair, Department of Repository and Research Services
- Chris Kelly, AFIP Public Affairs Director

Duke University Breast Specialized Program of Research Excellence (SPORE):
- Jeffrey Marks, Ph.D., Associate Professor, Surgery; co-creator, Duke University's Breast Tissue Repository

Mayo Clinic Prostate SPORE Tissue Procurement Core:
- Roxann Neuman, R.N., Urology Research Study Coordinator

University of Alabama at Birmingham Breast and Ovarian SPOREs:
- William Grizzle, M.D., Ph.D., Principal Investigator, Tissue Resources Core
- Katherine Sexton, Assistant Director, Tissue Collection and Banking Facility

University of Pittsburgh Health Sciences Tissue Bank (HSTB):
- Michael Becich, M.D., Ph.D., Chairman, Pathology, Shadyside Hospital; Director, Center for Pathology Informatics; Director, Benedum Oncology Informatics Center
- Rajiv Dhir, M.D., Director, Health Sciences Tissue Bank
- John Gilbertson, M.D., Director, Bioinformatics
- Ashok Patel, M.D.
- Michelle Bisceglia, HSTB Laboratory Manager

Ardais Corporation:
- Alan Buckler, Ph.D., Senior Vice President, R&D; Chief Scientific Officer
- Martin Ferguson, Ph.D., Senior Vice President, Bioinformatics
- Numerous other Ardais personnel

Genomics Collaborative, Inc.:
- Kevin Krenitsky, M.D., Senior Vice President; Medical Director
- Kristin Ardlie, Ph.D., Vice President, Genetics
- Scott Mahan, Laboratory Director

The authors would also like to thank the reviewers of this report for their insightful and timely reviews:
- Sheri Alpert, Ph.D., Adjunct Faculty, University of Notre Dame; medical privacy expert
- Lee Hilborne, M.D., M.P.H., Pathologist, University of California, Los Angeles; Adjunct Researcher, the RAND Corporation.

The authors would also like to thank several other people who contributed to this report:

- Gregory Downing, D.O., Ph.D., Director, Office of Technology and Industrial Relations, NCI; and Julie Schneider, D.Phil., Technology Program Manager, Office of Technology and Industrial Relations, NCI—for their valuable input both to the interview instrument and to draft versions of this report.
- William Trimble, RAND Research Assistant, who participated in the interviews with the University of Pittsburgh HSTB and the Mayo Clinic Prostate SPORE.
- Members of the NBN Design Team and Constella Health Sciences for their valuable input and suggestions to this study.
- Stephen Rattien, Ph.D., Debra Knopman, Ph.D., Lisa Sheldone, Lisa Spear, and others at RAND who provided support and expertise for this report.
- Jeri O'Donnell, who edited the manuscript; and Janet DeLand, who prepared the final copy.

Abbreviations

AACR	American Association for Cancer Research
AFIP	Armed Forces Institute of Pathology
AJCC	American Joint Committee on Cancer
API	application programming interface
BCR	Breast Cancer Registry
BIGR™	Biomaterials and Information for Genomic Research
BRAC	base realignment and closure
BRCA1	breast cancer 1 gene
BRCA2	breast cancer 2 gene
CCR	Coriell Cell Repositories
CCRP	Certified Career Research Professional
CDE	common data element
CFRs	Cancer Family Registries
CHTN	Cooperative Human Tissue Network
CPCTR	Cooperative Prostate Cancer Tissue Resource
DCC	Data Coordinating Center
DHHS	Department of Health and Human Services

DMCC	data management and coordination center
EDRN	Early Detection Research Network
ER/PR	estrogen receptor/progesterone receptor
FCCC	Fox Chase Cancer Center
FISH	fluorescence in situ hybridization
FTE	full-time equivalent
GCI	Genomics Collaborative, Inc.
H&E	hematoxylin and eosin (a commonly used histo-pathologic staining method)
HIPAA	Health Insurance Portability and Accountability Act
HSTB	Health Sciences Tissue Bank (University of Pittsburgh)
IATA	International Air Transport Association
ID	identification
IHC	immunohistochemistry
IP	intellectual property
IRB	institutional review board
IRC	Independent Review Consulting
ISBER	International Society for Biological and Environmental Repositories
IT	information technology
LAM	Lymphangioleiomyomatosis
LCMD	laser-capture micro-dissection
LIMS	Laboratory Information Management System
MTA	materials transfer agreement

NAACCR	North American Association of Central Cancer Registries, Inc.
NBAC	National Bioethics Advisory Commission
NBN	National Biospecimen Network
NCI	National Cancer Institute
NDC	National Dialogue on Cancer
NHGRI	National Human Genome Research Institute
NHLBI	National Heart, Lung, and Blood Institute
NIDDK	National Institute of Diabetes and Digestive and Kidney Diseases
NIH	National Institutes of Health
NIST	National Institute of Standards and Technology
NSABP	National Surgical Adjuvant Breast and Bowel Project
OCT	optimum cutting temperature (an embedding compound used in freezing specimens)
OHRP	Office for Human Research Protections
OR	operating room
OSD	organ specific database
OSU	Ohio State University
PCR	polymerase chain reaction
PI	principal investigator
QA	quality assurance
QC	quality control
RFA	Request for Application
RN	registered nurse
RT-PCR	reverse transcriptase polymerase chain reaction

SNOMED®	Systemized Nomenclature of Medicine
SNP	single nucleotide polymorphism
SOP	standard operating procedure
SPORE	Specialized Program of Research Excellence
TARP	Tissue Array Research Program
TAWG	Tissue Access Working Group
TMA	tissue microarrays
UAB	University of Alabama at Birmingham
UCI	University of California, Irvine
UPMC	University of Pittsburgh Medical Center

CHAPTER ONE

Introduction

Background

Human tissue has been stored for more than 100 years in the United States. An earlier RAND study conservatively estimated that there were more than 307 million tissue specimens from more than 178 million cases stored in the United States, accumulating at a rate of more than 20 million specimens per year (Eiseman and Haga, 1999). These tissue specimens are stored at military facilities, the National Institutes of Health (NIH) and its sponsored facilities, other federal agencies, state collection agencies (e.g., state forensic DNA banks and newborn screening laboratories), diagnostic pathology and cytology laboratories, university- and hospital-based research laboratories, commercial enterprises, and non-profit organizations. These tissue collections vary considerably, ranging from formal repositories to the informal storage of blood or tissue specimens in a researcher's freezer, and range in size from fewer than 200 to more than 92 million specimens.

The Armed Forces Institute of Pathology (AFIP) National Pathology Repository, the single largest tissue repository in the world, stores more than 92 million specimens. The tissue repositories supported by NIH are not as large as those at AFIP, but NIH is probably the largest funding source for tissue repositories. For instance, the National Cancer Institute (NCI) alone supports several major tissue resources, including the Cooperative Human Tissue Network

(CHTN), the Clinical Trials Cooperative Group Human Tissue Resources, the Early Detection Research Network (EDRN), the Cancer Family Registries (CFRs) for Breast and Ovarian Cancer and Colorectal Cancer, and the Specialized Programs of Research Excellence (SPOREs). The pathology departments at academic medical centers and community hospitals collectively constitute the largest and some of the oldest stores of biospecimens in the United States, with some specimens more than a century old. Finally, several private-sector companies maintain tissue banks for proprietary use, and others maintain banks for storage and distribution purposes.

The vast majority of tissue was originally collected for diagnostic or therapeutic reasons. Tissue specimens are also taken during autopsies performed to establish the cause of death. This tissue, which is largely stored at clinical and diagnostic laboratories and similar facilities, is sometimes used for research, educational, and quality control purposes, but the vast majority of it is not. Repositories have also been established specifically for research. In addition, several very large longitudinal studies collect and bank specimens from their study participants. Likewise, a fair amount of research simultaneously creates tissue collections or contributes to tissue banks. Other than for diagnostic purposes or research use, tissue is collected and stored for a variety of reasons, including blood transfusions, organ transplantation, procreative purposes (i.e., at sperm and embryo banks), identification (e.g., paternity testing, cases of abduction, or soldiers missing in action), and forensic purposes in criminal investigations.

Each institution that collects and stores human tissue was established to fulfill a specific set of objectives, and the design of each of these repositories is integrally linked to those objectives. Tissue collection, processing, and storage techniques vary depending on the purpose of the repository. For example, pathology laboratories that collect tissue from patients undergoing surgical or diagnostic procedures routinely store tissue in paraffin blocks, while some tissue collections established as part of research protocols are composed entirely of snap-frozen specimens. In addition, tissue specimens can be processed and stored in other formats, such as thin sections mounted on slides, cell cultures, or extracted DNA or RNA, depending on their intended use. Likewise, the quality and extent of information collected with the specimens can vary depending on the purpose for which the tissue was originally collected. Some repositories collect only pathologic characterizations of collected tissues; others collect extensive family histories and longitudinal data. The type of informed consent—whether general surgical consent or specific informed consent for the use of tissue for research purposes—also varies from repository to repository.

Many of the older repositories are valuable because of both the magnitude of their collections and the wealth of information they have collected about the specimens, information that may allow investigators to ascertain changes over time as environmental or societal shifts occur. However, these specimens may be of limited use for certain types of genomics- and proteomics-based research due to their age and/or the method in which they were stored (e.g., paraffin embedded instead of snap frozen). In addition, the lack of nationally agreed-upon quality control and standard operating procedures (SOPs) for the collection and storage of tissue may limit the usefulness of existing tissue collections for research requiring highly standardized specimen collection and preparation.

National Dialogue on Cancer

The National Dialogue on Cancer (NDC) is a forum that brings together representatives from the private sector, academia, non-profit organizations, and government agencies to foster and support efforts to "eradicate cancer as a major public health problem at the earliest possible time." A March 2002 meeting of the NDC Research Team was convened to explore approaches to optimize and accelerate the development of genomics- and proteomics-based diagnostics, treatments, and prevention strategies for cancer. Participants at this meeting identified "access to appropriately collected, consented, and annotated tissue" as a critical barrier to developing genomics-based therapies. Following this meeting, the Tissue Access Working Group (TAWG)—a self-selected group of individuals from the cancer research, drug development, delivery, commercialization, and patient advocacy sectors—was formed to address key barriers to biospecimen access.

The TAWG first met in August 2002 and concluded that the development of a national tissue resource and data bank was necessary if the nation was to ultimately realize the promise of genomics and proteomics for preventing and curing cancer as well as a range of other diseases. To help frame the issues at the August 2002 meeting, the TAWG reviewed the RAND Corporation's *Handbook of Human Tissue Sources: A National Resource of Human Tissue Samples* (Eiseman and Haga, 1999). The TAWG also discussed ways to include and utilize the valuable and available resources of currently existing biospecimen repositories described in the RAND report.

The TAWG, informed by several sources, including the United Kingdom's National Cancer Research Institute report entitled *Strategic Framework for Establishing a National Cancer Tissue Resource for Cancer Biology and Treatment Development*, and information from private tissue acquisition companies, identified the key goals and characteristics of a new model for a national biospecimen network (NBN). The overall goal of the TAWG is

> to establish a national, pre-competitive, regulatory compliant and genetic-privacy protected, standardized, inclusive, highest quality network of biological sample(s) banks; developed in partnerships with and supported by cancer survivors/advocates; shared, readily accessible, and searchable using appropriate informatics systems (e.g., amenable to molecular profiling capability).

A subset of the TAWG, the NBN Design Team, is currently in the process of developing a strategic plan—the NBN Design and Engineering Blueprint—to develop and implement the goals of the TAWG for a new NBN. In developing its blueprint, the team recognized that it was important to evaluate existing tissue resources to determine if any of them have the key characteristics of the NBN as defined by the TAWG, to identify "best practices" employed by existing repositories, and to assess whether any of these resources could be adapted to fulfill the requirements of the proposed NBN. To assist in their examination of existing tissue resources, the NBN Design Team requested that RAND conduct case studies of existing human tissue resources to evaluate their utility for genomics- and proteomics-based cancer research and that RAND identify "best practices" at these institutions.

RAND Study

Purpose

The purpose of the RAND study was to evaluate existing human tissue resources for their utility for genomics- and proteomics-based cancer research and to identify "best practices" at these institutions. Results of this study will be used to inform the NDC TAWG's strategic planning process to help guide the development of a new model for an NBN that will fulfill the needs of the research community.

Description of Study

RAND evaluated existing human tissue resources at twelve tissue repositories in the United States that represent a broad spectrum of repository types. The repositories were selected to represent resources funded primarily by the federal government or the private sector and are located at federal agencies, academic institutions, and private companies. Some of the repositories selected for evaluation contain specimens collected for diagnostic or therapeutic purposes; others contain specimens collected specifically as part of clinical research. Detailed descriptions of the repositories included in this study can be found in Chapter Two in the Methodology section.

RAND developed an interview instrument that asked questions about repository design, the bioinformatics system, privacy, ethical and legal issues, and public relations and marketing (see Chapter Two). RAND collected background information on repositories of interest and conducted site visits and interviews of key repository personnel. The interviews focused on the identification of best practices at each repository evaluated, such as innovative strategies, systems, and processes pertaining to specimen and data collection, storage, and distribution, as well as to bioinformatics systems and informed consent.

Organization of This Report

Chapter Two describes the methodology used to select the repositories to be evaluated and the development of the interview instrument. It also provides descriptions of each of the repositories evaluated for this study, and reasons why certain repositories were not included.

Chapter Three describes the various collection, processing, annotation, storage, and distribution procedures utilized by the repositories studied, plus their quality assurance, auditing, and standardized procedures. Chapter Four describes the bioinformatics and data management procedures used at the repositories; Chapter Five discusses consumer/user needs; Chapter Six covers the business plan and operations used by each repository; and Chapter Seven discusses privacy, ethical concerns, and consent issues that these repositories must address. Chapter Eight deals with intellectual property and other legal issues; and Chapter Nine describes public relations, marketing, and education efforts. Chapters Three through Nine also discuss and summarize best practices for each of these topics.

Chapter Ten details the RAND findings on best practices at each repository, as well as the best practices identified by RAND as necessary for establishing a national tissue resource and data bank to optimize and accelerate genomics- and proteomics-based research to develop diagnostics, treatments, and prevention strategies for cancer. The interview instrument is presented, in it entirety, in the Appendix.

Methodology

Selection of Repositories

RAND evaluated existing human tissue resources at several tissue repositories in the United States chosen to represent a broad spectrum of repository types and allow the description of a wide array of best practices that might be used by the National Biospecimen Network (NBN). RAND identified these repositories in conjunction with the sponsor to meet the criteria described below.

The repositories were selected to represent resources funded primarily by the federal government or the private sector and are located at federal agencies, academic institutions, and private companies. They also represent a range of operating models:

- Banking versus prospective collection and distribution
- Extensive versus little or no clinical/longitudinal data
- Networks versus individual sites
- Centralized versus decentralized tissue storage and bioinformatics
- Clinical trial/research participants (volunteers) versus patients not in clinical trials
- Specimens collected for diagnostic or therapeutics purposes versus specimens collected specifically for clinical research.

Repositories with important and unique collections or that are specifically involved in genomics/proteomics research were also selected.

Interviews

RAND identified the responsible individuals to be interviewed at each site and contacted them. In the majority of cases, in-person interviews with key personnel were set up at the repositories. A few interviews were conducted over the phone, and in some instances (identified below), repositories declined to participate in the study.

The RAND team developed a standardized interview instrument (see Appendix) and received input on the draft from the NBN Blueprint Design Team. The original instrument was based in part on information found in the following four documents:

1. Meeting summary from the National Dialogue on Cancer Research Team Tissue Access Working Group Two-Day Strategy Meeting, Washington, D.C., August 26–27, 2002.
2. Meeting summary from the National Dialogue on Cancer Research Team Tissue Access Working Group Meeting, Washington, D.C., January 7, 2003.
3. National Cancer Research Institute, "A Strategic Framework for Establishing a National Cancer Tissue Resource for Cancer Biology and Treatment Development," by Kirstine Knox and Cathy Ratcliffe at the National Translational Cancer Research Network Coordinating Centre, September 2002.
4. The RAND report *Handbook of Human Tissue Sources: A National Resource of Human Tissue Samples* (Eiseman and Haga, 1999).

The interview instrument focused on the key characteristics for a new national tissue repository model identified by the NDC TAWG:

- Biospecimen collection, processing, and storage
- Bioinformatics and data management
- Consumer/user needs
- Business plan and operations
- Privacy, ethical concerns, and consent issues
- Intellectual property and legal issues
- Public relations, marketing, and education.

The interviews asked about quality control, auditing, and standardization in each of the areas listed above. The focus was on identifying best practices at each repository, such as innovative strategies, systems, and processes pertaining to specimen and data collection, storage, and distribution, and to bioinformatics systems and informed consent. The original interview instrument was modified slightly after input provided during initial interviews with Ardais and the Cooperative Human Tissue Network (CHTN).

In most cases, two members of the research team conducted each site visit and interview. Notes from each interview were then prepared and reviewed by the interviewers, and the interviewees were given an opportunity to comment on or correct any of the information documented from the interview. These notes were then presented to the entire RAND research team for analysis. Following completion of the interviews, each section of the interview instrument was assigned to a RAND team member to analyze across the repositories and to identify best practices. Then a second team member evaluated this analysis as it related specifically to best practices.

It should be noted that the level of participation by the repository personnel interviewed varied significantly. RAND usually made the interview request to one of the principal individuals involved in the repository, and it was up to that person to include other repository personnel in the interview process. In some instances, RAND interviewed a wide range of those involved in the repository process (e.g., at Ardais and University of Pittsburgh Medical Center); in other instances, however, only one individual was interviewed (e.g., at Duke University Breast SPORE and Mayo Clinic Prostate SPORE). Therefore, the level of detailed information provided by the repositories was uneven in terms of the types and numbers of individuals who participated in the interview process. For example, often times there was no representation from the information technology side of the process, in which case the information provided by the repository principals on the bioinformatics system was usually quite generalized.

Repositories Evaluated

The repositories evaluated were grouped into three general categories. The first category, government, includes two repositories funded by and operated by federal agencies, one repository contracted by a federal agency, and three repositories funded through Cooperative Agreements with a federal agency. The second category, academia, includes repositories at three major academic medical centers that are funded through Specialized Center Grants (P50s) from the National Cancer Institute (NCI), and one repository at a major academic medical center that houses both NCI-funded resources and institute-funded programs. The third category, industry, includes two private companies that operate biospecimen repositories.

All of the repositories evaluated are summarized in Table 2.1 and described in detail, including their history, funding mechanism, and objectives, in the following subsections.

Government

National Cancer Institute
NCI at the National Institutes of Health (NIH) supports numerous tissue resources, including the NCI Cooperative Group Human Tissue Resources, CHTN, the Early Detection Research Network (EDRN), the Specialized Programs of Research Excellence (SPOREs), and NCI intramural collections. The evaluation of NCI-supported tissue resources entailed gathering background information about all the tissue resources using the Internet and available literature, performing site visits and interviews at representative repositories (e.g., CHTN, EDRN, and the Tissue Array Research Program [TARP]), and interviewing key personnel involved in coordinating NCI's cancer specimen resources.

Cooperative Human Tissue Network. Roger Aamodt, Ph.D., Chief, Resources Development Branch, Cancer Diagnosis Program, at NCI first developed the concept for a network that would supply human

Table 2.1
Repositories Evaluated

Repository	Interviewees	Date of Interview
Government		
National Institutes of Health		
National Cancer Institute		
Cooperative Human Tissue Network	Roger Aamodt, PhD, Chief, Resources Development Branch, NCI; Marianna Bledsoe, Program Director, NCI	6/17/2003
Cooperative Human Tissue Network Eastern Division	Virginia LiVolsi, MD, Principal Investigator; Kelly Feil, Director; Dee McGarvey, Manager	7/24/2003
Tissue Array Research Program	Stephen M. Hewitt, MD, PhD, Director, TARP	6/30/2003
Early Detection Research Network	Sudhir Srivastava, PhD, MPH, Program Director, EDRN Coordination Office; Donald Johnsey, EDRN Information Technology Manager	7/3/2003
Philadelphia Familial Breast Cancer Registry	Mary Daly, MD, PhD, Principal Investigator; Jeanne Beck, PhD, Director, Coriell Cell Repositories	8/4/2003
National Heart Lung and Blood Institute	Kathi Shea, Director, Repository Operations (BBI Biotech); Susan Sherer, Senior Study Coordinator (Cleveland Clinic)	6/26/2003
Department of Defense		
Armed Forces Institute of Pathology	Francis Gannon, MD, Chair, Department of Repository and Research Services; Chris Kelly, Public Affairs Director	7/21/2003

Table 2.1 (continued)

Repository	Interviewees	Date of Interview
Academia		
Duke University Breast SPORE	Jeffrey Marks, PhD, Assoc. Professor Surgery	8/12/2003
Mayo Clinic Prostate SPORE	Roxann Neumann, RN, Urology Research Study Coordinator	8/6/2003
University of Alabama at Birmingham Breast and Ovarian SPOREs	William Grizzle, MD, PhD, Principal Investigator, Tissue Resources Core	8/7/2003
University of Pittsburgh Medical Center (CPCTR, EDRN, Lung SPORE)	Michael Becich, MD, PhD, Pathology Chairman, Director, Informatics; Rajiv Dhir, MD, Director, Health Sciences Tissue Bank; John Gilbertson, MD, Director, Bioinformatics; Ashook Patel, MD; Michelle Bisceglia, HSTB Laboratory Manager	7/18/2003
Industry		
Ardais Corporation	Alan Buckler, PhD, Senior VP, R&D, Chief Scientific Officer; Martin Ferguson, PhD, Senior VP, Bioinformatics; other Ardais personnel[a]	6/16/2003
Genomics Collaborative, Inc.	Kevin Krenitsky, MD, Senior VP, Medical Director; Kristin Ardlie, PhD, VP, Genetics; Scott Mahan, Laboratory Director	7/30/2003

[a]RAND's interview and site visit with Ardais Corporation was in conjunction with a site visit by representatives from the NDC TAWG and NCI.

tissue specimens for the conduct of basic and developmental cancer research in the mid-1980s. As a result, in 1987, CHTN was founded in response to a Request for Application (RFA) at three institutions under Cooperative Agreements with NCI. The University of Pennsylvania/National Disease Research Interchange, the University of Alabama at Birmingham (UAB), and Ohio State University (OSU) constituted the initial network. The Children's Cancer Study Group provided pediatric tumor specimens under a subcontract with OSU.

In January 1991, CHTN expanded to five divisions, including the direct funding of the Children's Cancer Study Group as the CHTN Pediatric Division at the Children's Hospital of Columbus, Ohio, and Case Western Reserve University. Currently, CHTN is made up of six divisions:

1. Eastern Division: University of Pennsylvania—responsible for the area of the northeast bounded by the western and southern borders of Pennsylvania, as well as Delaware, Alaska, and Hawaii.
2. Mid-Atlantic Division: Medical Center University of Virginia—responsible for Maryland, Virginia, and the District of Columbia.
3. Midwestern Division: Ohio State University—includes West Virginia and states west of Pennsylvania north to Minnesota and south through Missouri, and Canada.
4. Southern Division: University of Alabama at Birmingham—encompasses Kentucky and all states south and west from the Carolinas to Texas.
5. Western Division: Vanderbilt University Medical Center—covers all states north of Oklahoma and west of Texas.
6. Pediatric Division: Columbus Children's Hospital—provides childhood tumors and diseased and normal tissue nationwide.

CHTN uses a prospective specimen procurement model to meet the needs of basic and developmental researchers. CHTN primarily collects and distributes surgical and autopsy specimens. These specimens are provided to researchers along with basic pathologic, histological, and demographic data. Dr. Aamodt and Marianna Bledsoe,

Program Director, Resources Development Branch, Cancer Diagnosis Program, NCI, were interviewed about the practices and procedures of the overall network. Virginia LiVolsi, M.D., Principal Investigator; Kelly Feil, Director; and Dee McGarvey, Manager, at CHTN Eastern Division, University of Pennsylvania, were interviewed specifically about the Eastern Division.

Tissue Array Research Program. In 1999, Richard Klausner, M.D., then Director of NCI, started to develop a research program that would utilize tissue microarray technology developed by Olli Kallioniemi and colleagues at the National Human Genome Research Institute (NHGRI). TARP was conceived as a joint program (i.e., a collaborative effort) by NCI and NHGRI. NCI produced the tissue microarrays that were to be distributed extramurally by the Eastern Division of CHTN (see above for a description of CHTN), while NHGRI was to be responsible for development of the tissue microarray technology. Since that time, the NHGRI laboratory involved in developing tissue microarray technology has ceased to exist, and the TARP laboratory has expanded to produce and develop the technology. TARP was originally in the Office of the Director, NCI, but moved to the Centers for Cancer Research.

The primary objective of TARP is to develop and disseminate tissue microarrays containing samples of multiple tumors (300 to 500 tissues per array) to cancer researchers to expedite the discovery of novel cancer targets for the detection, treatment, and prevention of cancer. These microarrays provide a tool for high-throughput screening of multiple tumor tissues with immunohistochemistry, in situ hybridization, and fluorescence in situ hybridization (FISH). Stephen M. Hewitt, M.D., Ph.D., Director of TARP at NCI, was interviewed.

Early Detection Research Network. EDRN was initiated by NCI in 1998 to improve methods for detecting the signatures of cancer cells. EDRN is funded through peer-reviewed Cooperative Agreements. It is a consortium for collaborative research to link the discovery of biomarkers directly to the next steps in the process of developing early detection tests. This network brings together researchers across disciplines and institutions to identify, develop, and validate bio-markers. Network participants act as a team in a streamlined process through a distributed physical network of geographically dispersed repositories with a centralized bioinformatics and data management system. The network primarily consists of approximately 40 research universities but also includes more than a dozen private companies as industry partners. Sudhir Srivastava, Ph.D., M.P.H., Program Direc-tor of the EDRN Coordination Office; and Donald Johnsey, EDRN Information Technology Manager, were interviewed.

Philadelphia Familial Breast Cancer Registry. In 1995, the Philadel-phia Familial Breast Cancer Registry, part of the Breast and Ovarian Cancer Family Registries (CFRs),[1] was established at the Fox Chase Cancer Center (FCCC) as part of a multisite/international breast cancer registry for familial breast cancer. It was created through a Cooperative Agreement with the NCI Division of Cancer Control and Population Sciences. This grant was used by FCCC to build on a smaller registry designed to study breast cancer funded by the Department of Defense.

Philadelphia Familial Breast Cancer Registry is now one of six sites designed as a resource for breast and ovarian cancer research that includes extensive epidemiological medical data on breast and ovarian cancer patients and their family members; and biospecimens, includ-ing blood, and whenever possible, tumor specimens. Data are gath-ered longitudinally and placed in a central location at the University of California, Irvine (UCI) to make them available to the research com-munity. The six sites are:

1. Philadelphia Familial Breast Cancer Registry—at Fox Chase Cancer Center and the Coriell Institute for Medical Research.
2. Australian Breast Cancer Family Registry—at the University of Melbourne and the Peter MacCallum Cancer Institute.

---

[1] This was formerly called the Cooperative Family Registry for Breast Cancer Studies.

3. Metropolitan New York Registry of Breast Cancer Families—at the Joseph L. Mailman School of Public Health and Columbia University.
4. Northern California Cooperative Family Registry—at the Northern California Cancer Center and Stanford University School of Medicine.
5. Ontario Registry for Studies of Familial Breast Cancer—at Cancer Care Ontario.
6. Utah Cooperative Breast Cancer Registry—at the Utah Health Sciences Center.

Biospecimen collection is handled at each CFR site. The Philadelphia Familial Cancer Registry, Northern California Cooperative Family Registry, and Utah Cooperative Breast Cancer Registry all use the Coriell Cell Repositories (CCR) for storage. CCR stores several collections, most of which are sponsored by the federal government. Other sponsors include foundations and voluntary health organizations. CCR receives blood, skin biopsies, and other tissue and establishes viable, uncontaminated cell lines from them for distribution to the research community. CCR has transformed some of the lymphocytes from the CFRs into cell lines to provide a perpetual source of DNA.

The grant was renewed in FY 2000 for a second five-year cycle. The six sites now focus on doing research as opposed to the initial focus on collecting the resource. Mary Daly, M.D., Ph.D., Principal Investigator of the Philadelphia Familial Breast Cancer Registry, and Jeanne Beck, Ph.D., Professor at the Coriell Institute for Medical Research, Director of the Coriell Cell Repositories, were interviewed, the former in person and the latter by phone.

National Heart, Lung, and Blood Institute
The NHLBI Biological Specimen Repository, established in 1974, contains over 3 million specimens available for use by researchers for studies related to transfusion-transmitted diseases, other blood disorders, lung diseases, and diseases of the cardiovascular system. The

NHLBI Biological Specimen Repository also contains clinical, epidemiologic, virologic, and serologic information associated with the specimens.

BBI Biotech is under contract with NHLBI to store specimens for thirteen NHLBI studies, the largest one being the Retroviral Epidemiological Study, which is geared around blood transfusions. BBI also stores specimens for the NHLBI-sponsored Lymphangioleiomyomatosis (LAM) Registry, which is a national registry of patients with LAM, a rare lung disease characterized by an unusual type of muscle cell that invades the tissue of the lungs, including the airways, and blood and lymph vessels. The LAM Registry is the only NHLBI collection that banks both blood and tissue specimens, including serum, plasma, RNA, DNA, and tissue. In addition to the collections held for NHLBI, BBI is storing specimens from approximately 700 different NCI studies and two Hepatitis C trials that are sponsored by the National Institute of Diabetes and Digestive and Kidney Diseases (NIDDK).

BBI was originally established in 1973 to provide a service to researchers running large trials involving specimen collection and specimen storage. It merged with Cambridge Biosciences to become BBI in 1992. BBI became the repository for NHLBI in 1998 after successfully winning a proposal solicitation. NCI has been using BBI to store specimens since 1973.

Kathi Shea, Director of Repository Operations, and Susan Sherer, Senior Study Coordinator, LAM Registry Data Coordinating Center, Cleveland Clinic, were interviewed, the former in person and the latter by e-mail. In addition, RAND evaluated the tissue repository at BBI and the practices and procedures of the NHLBI LAM study in particular.

Armed Forces Institute of Pathology (AFIP) National Pathology Repository

The National Pathology Repository, located at AFIP (a tri-service agency of the Department of Defense), has the single largest and most comprehensive collection of pathology material in the world. Since 1864, this repository has collected more than 2.8 million cases comprising more than 50 million microscopic slides, 30 million paraffin tissue blocks, 12 million preserved wet tissue specimens, and associated written records. The repository currently accessions approximately 60,000 new cases per year representing both sexes, all races and ethnicities, and all ages from contributors worldwide.

AFIP was established at the end of the Civil War to examine battlefield specimens and as a medical museum. In 1943, AFIP's main mission evolved from acting as a museum to serving as a pathology institute. Currently, AFIP primarily serves as a secondary referral resource for expert diagnosis or confirmation of a diagnosis, although 25 percent of cases come to AFIP in need of an initial diagnosis. Included are veterinary pathology cases—animal tissue not previously reviewed by a veterinary pathologist. AFIP also receives thousands of special registry cases each year, including Persian Gulf War Illness, Prisoner of War, and cases sent from military hospitals closed in the base realignment and closure (BRAC) process. AFIP's main purpose is to provide clinical diagnostic pathology support to the Armed Services, but it performs the same services for the civilian sector. Researchers at AFIP also perform long-term epidemiological research.

Francis Gannon, M.D., Chair of the Department of Repository and Research Services, and Chris Kelly, AFIP Public Affairs Director, were interviewed to evaluate the tissue resources at the AFIP National Pathology Repository.

Academia

Specialized Programs of Research Excellence (SPOREs)

NCI established the SPOREs in 1992. Their purpose is to "promote interdisciplinary research and to speed the bi-directional exchange between basic and clinical science to move basic research findings from the laboratory to applied settings involving patients and populations" (SPORE Web site: http://spores.nci.nih.gov). SPOREs are funded through Specialized Center Grants (P50s). Currently, NCI is funding SPOREs on breast, ovarian, prostate, lung, gastrointestinal, genitourinary, brain, skin, head, and neck cancers, and lymphoma.

The goal of the SPOREs is "to bring to clinical care settings novel ideas that have the potential to reduce cancer incidence and mortality, improve survival, and to improve the quality of life." The idea is to have basic researchers in the laboratories work with clinical scientists to conduct collaborative research in the areas of cancer prevention, detection, diagnosis, treatment, and control. As part of this effort, each SPORE establishes specialized resources, including tissue resource and bioinformatics cores.

Several SPOREs were chosen for inclusion in this study: the Duke University Breast SPORE, the Mayo Clinic Prostate SPORE, the University of Alabama at Birmingham (UAB) Breast and Ovarian SPOREs, the Johns Hopkins University Lymphoma SPORE, and the Vanderbilt University Breast, Gastrointestinal, and Lung SPOREs. Interviews were conducted with individuals at the Duke University, the Mayo Clinic, and UAB responsible for managing the tissue resource core for the SPOREs at their institutions. Brief descriptions of the SPOREs where interviews were conducted are directly below. An explanation for why some SPOREs initially selected for this study were not evaluated can be found in the next section of this chapter.

Duke University Breast SPORE. Duke University initially received funding for a Breast SPORE in 1995. It then lost funding for the SPORE in 2001 but was recently re-funded, in July 2003. The Tissue Resource Core is an integrated part of a pre-existing repository established by a molecular biology researcher and a surgeon in 1987. Jeffrey Marks, Ph.D., Associate Professor, Surgery, and co-creator of Duke University's Breast Tissue Repository, was interviewed by phone about the Duke University Breast SPORE tissue resource.

Mayo Clinic Prostate SPORE. Mayo Clinic Prostate SPORE was established in 2001. The goal of the program is to identify genetic susceptibility factors for prostate cancer that can improve the understanding of the etiology of the disease and potentially identify men at increased risk of developing prostate cancer for whom prevention strategies might be targeted.

The Prostate Cancer Tissue Procurement Core of Mayo Clinic Prostate SPORE is an integrated part of an ongoing program at the Mayo Clinic to collect, process, and store tissue from prostate cancer patients. The goal of the Tissue Procurement Core is to procure prostate tissue from every prostate cancer patient undergoing radical prostatectomy at the Mayo Clinic. The Tissue Procurement Core is also electronically integrated with the Prostate Cancer Patient Registry and the Biostatistics Core to provide investigators with clinically annotated specimens. Roxann Neuman, R.N., Urology Research Study Coordinator, was interviewed by phone about the Mayo Clinic Prostate SPORE Tissue Procurement Core.

University of Alabama at Birmingham Breast and Ovarian SPOREs. The UAB Breast SPORE, established in 2001, is focused on the areas of breast cancer prevention, including genetics, chemoprevention, and therapy. The UAB Ovarian SPORE, established in 1999, is focused on areas of gene therapy, targeted immunotherapy, and chemoprevention for ovarian cancer. Both SPOREs compliment ongoing programs at the UAB Comprehensive Cancer Center in the areas of breast and ovarian cancer. UAB also has a newly funded Pancreatic SPORE. A Brain SPORE with an associated tissue resource is not associated with the breast, ovarian, and pancreatic tissue resources.

The UAB Breast and Ovarian SPOREs Tissue Resource Cores are integrated with pre-existing shared facilities at the UAB Comprehensive Cancer Center. Since 1987, UAB has been a member of CHTN, serving as the Southern Division (see description of CHTN, above). Thus, UAB has extensive experience in collecting, processing, storing, and distributing a wide range of human tissue to support research. The goal of the UAB Breast and Ovarian SPOREs Tissue Resource Cores is to collect well-characterized breast and ovarian tumor specimens and matching adjacent specimens, along with clinical and demographic information, for use by SPORE members and by selected extramural users for special research purposes. William Grizzle, M.D., Ph.D., Principal Investigator of the Tissue Resources Core, was interviewed by phone about the UAB Breast and Ovarian SPOREs tissue resources.

University of Pittsburgh Medical Center

The Health Sciences Tissue Bank (HSTB) at the University of Pittsburgh initially started banking tissues as a resource for researchers at the university, but the program has grown to include NCI-funded resources (the Cooperative Prostate Cancer Tissue Resource [CPCTR], an EDRN Gastrointestinal grant, and a Lung SPORE), and institute-funded programs (a melanoma banking program and a cancer biomarkers laboratory). HSTB also prospectively banks a variety of neoplasms, with special emphasis in the areas of breast, lung, urologic, and head and neck neoplasms. The banking of prostate specimens was started in 1991 by Michael Becich, M.D., Ph.D.; and CPCTR, of which Dr. Becich and Rajiv Dhir, M.D., are Co-Principal Investigators, was funded three years ago. The banking, directed by Dr. Dhir, occurs at four main academic University of Pittsburgh Medical Center (UPMC) hospitals in Pittsburgh, including Magee-Women's Hospital of UPMC, UPMC Presbyterian, UPMC Shadyside, and Children's Hospital of Pittsburgh of UPMC.

Dr. Becich is also Co-Principal Investigator of the Pennsylvania Cancer Alliance Bioinformatics Consortium, a group of six cancer research centers in Pennsylvania that has been funded to develop "a statewide serum and tissue repository, a data model for biomarker data storage, a statewide model for bioinformatics, a public access website for disseminating research results, and a strategic plan to support aggressive collaboration between industry and academia" (http://pcabc.upmc.edu/).

Dr. Becich, Chairman of Pathology at UPMC Shadyside, Director of the Center for Pathology Informatics, and the Benedum Oncology Informatics Center; Dr. Dhir, Director of Genitourinary Pathology and of the University of Pittsburgh HSTB; John Gilbertson, M.D., Director of Bioinformatics; Ashok Patel, M.D.; and Michelle Bisceglia, Manager of the HSTB Laboratory, were interviewed during a site visit to UPMC Shadyside.

Industry

Ardais Corporation

Ardais Corporation is a private clinical genomics company that grew out of a mutual interest among researchers at Duke University Medical Center and Ardais founders to develop a tissue/data banking center that could simultaneously support the needs of Duke internal researchers and the broader research community. Ardais, in collaboration with its network of partner medical institutions, launched the National Clinical Genomics Initiative in September 2000, after obtaining initial funding in December 1999, to facilitate genomics-based biomedical research among academic and industrial researchers. The goals of the initiative are to develop systematic, large-scale procedures to comprehensively collect, process, and store research quality clinical materials and associated information; to provide these resources in optimized formats for biomedical research; and to support the research and clinical programs at participating medical institutions. Ardais has established best practices working groups to provide advice, continually review, and ensure that operations are ethically appropriate, technically excellent, and practical.

Alan Buckler, Ph.D., Senior Vice President of Research & Development, Chief Scientific Officer; Martin Ferguson, Ph.D., Senior Vice President of Bioinformatics; and numerous other individuals were interviewed on site as part of the NCI/NDC and RAND site visit to evaluate the tissue resources at Ardais.

Genomics Collaborative, Inc. (GCI)

GCI was established in 1998 primarily as a for-profit private biotechnology research company designed to participate in and facilitate the application of genetic research to drug and diagnostic discovery decisions. Specimen collection began in earnest in March 2000 to collect multiple types of specimens (e.g., tissue, serum, and DNA) on the same patient, along with detailed medical and demographic information. GCI's approach links human genes, proteins, and clinical outcomes through proprietary technology platforms. GCI offers human DNA, RNA, sera, and snap-frozen tissue specimens linked to detailed medical information collected from patient populations worldwide. GCI personnel provide expertise in designing and conducting human genetic studies geared toward the development of therapeutics and diagnostics. They also offer high-throughput analysis tools, including single nucleotide polymorphism (SNP) genotyping, DNA sequencing, reverse transcriptase polymerase chain reaction (RT-PCR), and gene expression analyses.

GCI uses a dual business model. It has a fee-for-service side that works primarily with the pharmaceutical industry to design and collect specimens for drug development. The other side of the business participates in larger collaborative programs with pharmaceutical companies, biotech companies, and academic and government institutions.

Kevin Krenitsky, M.D., Senior Vice President, Medical Director; Kristin Ardlie, Ph.D., Vice President, Genetics; and Scott Mahan, Laboratory Director, were interviewed.

Repositories Not Included in the Evaluation

Several repositories originally selected for inclusion in this study were not evaluated. The reasons are as follows:

SPOREs

It was not possible to schedule interviews with the Johns Hopkins University Lymphoma SPORE and the Vanderbilt University Breast, Gastrointestinal, and Lung SPOREs. The Lymphoma SPORE at Johns Hopkins University was established in 2002, and the Principal Investigator indicated that the SPORE would be better able to discuss best practices in six months when the program was more established, putting an interview outside the time frame of this study. The Director of Tissue Profiling Informatics at the Vanderbilt-Ingram Cancer Center, Vanderbilt University Medical Center, was contacted about participating in the study; however, it was not possible to schedule an interview within the time frame of this study.

IMPATH Inc.

IMPATH Inc., a private company formed in 1988 to improve outcomes for cancer patients by providing cancer information and analyses, was identified because it has a database of over one million patient profiles and outcomes data on over 2.3 million individuals and because it represents a for-profit repository model. The Vice President and Scientific Director at IMPATH was initially eager to participate in the study; however, once the interview request was referred to the legal department, the process was held up over concerns about proprietary issues. The Scientific Director was not able to arrange for the necessary approvals from IMPATH legal and management in time to be included in the interview process.

National Surgical Adjuvant Breast and Bowel Project (NSABP)

NSABP is a clinical-trials cooperative group supported by NCI that focuses on breast and colorectal cancer studies. The NSABP tissue repository has collected tumors and matching adjacent tissue from more than 50,000 women and men at almost 200 major medical centers, university hospitals, large oncology practice groups, and health maintenance organizations, and has distributed them to investigators. The Chief Executive Officer of NSABP indicated that there was an ongoing independent audit of NSABP and that as a result, tissue collection practices might be altered substantially in the near future. Therefore, she declined to participate in the study.

Program for Critical Technologies in Molecular Medicine

The Program for Critical Technologies in Molecular Medicine is a shared resource of the Yale Cancer Center within the Department of Pathology at Yale University School of Medicine. The program, established in 1992, is a collaborative core laboratory set up for state-of-the-art histologic, genetic, and molecular analysis of human tumors to complement clinical studies in prevention, diagnosis, and treatment of cancer. More than 10,000 frozen specimens have been collected for research purposes, and more than 3 million archived paraffin blocks from clinical cases are available.

The leaders of the repository recently changed. Although they were willing to be interviewed, they stated that they had recently experienced a variety of problems related to the Health Insurance Portability and Accountability Act (HIPAA), personnel changes, and tissue costs that have limited their effectiveness. Overall, they did not think their current operations would yield any "best practices." Therefore, the Program for Critical Technologies in Molecular Medicine was not evaluated for this study.

Determining "Best Practices"

Best practices were determined and agreed upon by the RAND research team based on the findings at the twelve repositories evaluated and the goal of the NBN Design Team to establish a national network of biospecimen repositories to collect, process, store, and distribute appropriately consented diseased and normal tissue with associated clinical data supported and coordinated by an accessible, searchable, and minable bioinformatics system. Best practices were defined as strategies, systems, processes, and methodologies that should be used by a repository to provide a robust resource for genomics- and proteomics-based research in the areas of biospecimen and data collection, storage, and distribution; bioinformatics and data management; meeting the needs of researchers; business plan and operations; ethical and legal issues; and public relations, marketing, and education.

Types of Information Not Shared

The interviewees in all cases were forthcoming about almost all information requested by RAND. There were, however, a few incidents where repositories declined to share specific information. For instance, both GCI and Ardais declined to provide cost information (costs of collecting, storing, and distribution, as well as prices they charge for tissue and tissue-related services). CHTN Eastern Division did not share the names of its specimen-source satellite institutions, because it did not want to jeopardize the special relationships it had developed with these institutions.

CHAPTER THREE

Biospecimen Collection, Processing, Annotation, Storage, and Distribution

Each biospecimen repository evaluated for this study was established to fulfill a specific set of objectives, and the design of each repository is integrally linked to those objectives. Techniques for tissue collection, processing, annotation, and storage—the core functions of a biospecimen repository—vary depending on the purpose for which the repository was established. Likewise, the quality and extent of information collected with the specimens vary depending on the purpose for which the tissue was originally collected. Details about biospecimen collection, processing, annotation, storage, and distribution at each repository evaluated and the best practices identified are described in this chapter.

Biospecimen Collection

Tissue Sources
All twelve of the repositories collect tissue that was originally removed for routine medical care, such as surgery, or other diagnostic or medical procedures. Five of the repositories (EDRN, Philadelphia Familial Breast Cancer Registry, NHLBI, University of Pittsburgh HSTB, and GCI) also collect specimens from people who volunteer to participate in clinical trials, registries, or other research projects. Table 3.1 provides a profile of the tissue sources for the twelve repositories evaluated.

Table 3.1
Tissue Source Profile

Repository	Tissue Source (patients vs. volunteers)	Reason for Tissue Removal	Demographic Distribution		
			Minority Populations	Children	Other Countries
CHTN	Patients	Surgery; autopsy; organ donation; clinical laboratory specimens (e.g., blood, sera, ascites, and cytology samples)	Yes	Yes	No
TARP	Patients	Surgery; autopsy	Yes	Yes	Yes (collaborative studies in Poland, China)
EDRN	Volunteers and patients	Clinical trials; other research	Yes	Yes	Yes (UK, Canada, Israel)
Philadelphia Familial Breast Cancer Registry	Volunteers (breast or ovarian cancer patients or participants in the "high risk" cancer program) and family members	Epidemiological research; surgery	Yes	No (not yet)	Yes

Table 3.1 (continued)

Repository	Tissue Source (patients vs. volunteers)	Reason for Tissue Removal	Demographic Distribution		
			Minority Populations	Children	Other Countries
NHLBI[a]	Volunteers	Epidemiological research; surgery (lung tissue and other LAM-related tissue types)	LAM—not specifically	No	Yes (Canada, South America)
AFIP	Patients	Surgery; autopsy	Yes	Yes	Yes
Duke University Breast SPORE	Patients	Surgery	Yes—based on the population in the Duke area	No	No
Mayo Clinic Prostate SPORE	Patients	Surgery	Yes—based on the population in Rochester, MN	No	No
UAB Breast and Ovarian SPOREs	Patients	Surgery	Yes—based on the population in Birmingham, AL	No	No

Table 3.1 (continued)

Repository	Tissue Source (patients vs. volunteers)	Reason for Tissue Removal	Demographic Distribution		
			Minority Populations	Children	Other Countries
University of Pittsburgh HSTB	Mostly patients; some volunteers	Surgery; autopsies of cancer patients (metastases); organ donation (normal controls); clinical trials (~5%)	Yes—based on the population in Pittsburgh, PA	Yes	No
Ardais	Patients	Surgery	Yes—based on the population at four collection sites	No (IRB approvals are in place)	No
GCI	Patients and volunteers	Surgery (tissue specimens); blood banks (DNA and sera)	Yes	No	Yes (Belgium, Poland, Tunisia, Vietnam, India)

[a]Demographic information about the sources of the specimens is kept by the NHLBI study managers and not with the specimens at BBI.

Some of the repositories actively recruit individuals to contribute tissue to their repositories (Philadelphia Familial Breast Cancer Registry, University of Pittsburgh HSTB, Ardais, and GCI). Mayo Clinic Prostate SPORE identifies potential sources of tissue after the surgery has occurred and the pathologists have reviewed the tissue. AFIP primarily receives specimens from pathologists at other institutions requesting a second opinion.

CHTN, TARP, AFIP, and University of Pittsburgh HSTB also collect tissue from autopsy. CHTN collects normal tissue (for comparison with diseased tissue) from autopsy and from organ transplantation—both normal organs not suitable for transplant purposes and the diseased organs that were removed. Likewise, University of Pittsburgh HSTB collects normal tissue from organ donors who consent to donate their organs for research. University of Pittsburgh HSTB also has a Warm Autopsy Program, in which it collects specimens of metastatic tumors from autopsies performed within hours of death on cancer patients (mainly prostate cancer patients living in hospice care) who have consented before dying.

EDRN, Philadelphia Familial Breast Cancer Registry, and NHLBI primarily collect specimens specifically for research purposes. However, the NHLBI LAM Registry and the Philadelphia Familial Breast Cancer Registry also collect surgical specimens of diseased tissue.

Biospecimen collection by CHTN is request driven. Therefore, CHTN collects specific types of tissue in response to the needs of researchers. CHTN obtains tissue primarily from surgical patients. It also collects some cytological and clinical laboratory (e.g., blood and serum) biospecimens. Some tissue is collected from organ transplantations—both normal organs that could not be used for transplant purposes (particularly eyes)—and the diseased organs that were removed. Some tissue is also collected from autopsy. On occasion, there are private donors who voluntarily donate tissue, blood, and/or urine. In addition, some tissue is collected from individuals who are participants in clinical trials. Some CHTN divisions also have the ability to recruit volunteers if researchers were to request this service.[1]

The tissue used to make the TARP microarrays that are distributed to the research community comes mainly from CHTN. The tissue is primarily tumors from cancer patients and normal tissue from patients with diseases other than cancer. TARP also builds tissue microarrays as part of collaborative research, and tissue comes from such diverse sources as the NIH Clinical Center, Poland, China, and U.S. and international cooperative groups. Specimens used to make the tissue microarrays for collaborative studies are supplied by the collaborators.

EDRN, Philadelphia Familial Breast Cancer Registry, and NHLBI recruit volunteers for tissue donation as part of their participation in clinical trials, as members of disease-specific registries, or for other types of research. The tissue sources for EDRN are volunteers who have agreed to be part of clinical trials or other research. Similarly, NHLBI LAM tissue sources are study volunteers or LAM patients who have enrolled in the LAM Registry. In addition to the LAM Registry, the LAM Foundation helps to recruit tissue sources. Philadelphia Familial Breast Cancer Registry recruits families through several sources. A proband (a patient with breast or ovarian cancer) or someone with a very strong family history of breast or ovarian cancer (FCCC has a very large "high risk" program for cancer) is identified first, and then Philadelphia Familial Breast Cancer Registry tries to enroll additional family members. Philadelphia Familial Breast Cancer Registry also networks with several community hospitals that refer participants. Tissue comes from breast and ovarian cancer patients, participants in the "high risk" program, volunteers, and family members.

Tissue collected by AFIP is primarily from surgical patients. However, AFIP does not recruit tissue sources. AFIP is a referral service to primary pathologists, and it is the pathologist who submits the specimen.

---

[1] Consent issues relevant to biospecimen collection, storage, annotation, and distribution are discussed for each repository in Chapter Seven.

Duke University Breast SPORE primarily collects tissue from patients undergoing breast biopsies or surgery for breast cancer. Occasionally, normal breast tissue is collected for specific projects. Likewise, the UAB Breast and Ovarian SPOREs collect tissue from patients undergoing surgery for breast or ovarian cancer. Nurses in the breast and gynecology oncology clinics at UAB identify patients that are eligible for Breast SPORE and Ovarian SPORE protocols and obtain informed consent from those patients. Information about which patients consented to participate in the SPORE protocols is communicated with the SPOREs prior to surgery. Normal and diseased tissues are also collected for the UAB SPOREs for use as controls for the cancer specimens.

Mayo Clinic Prostate SPORE collects tissue from patients undergoing either radical or supra-pubic prostatectomy. Tissue sources are identified after the tissue is received in the pathology laboratory, a frozen section analysis has been done, and the pathologist has verified that there is tissue available for research. A registered nurse working for the SPORE is notified that tissue was collected and then visits the patient in the hospital room within 24 hours after the surgery to obtain consent for use of the tissue for research purposes. At University of Pittsburgh HSTB, tissue is primarily from cancer patients. Normal prostate and bladder tissue is also collected from organ donors, and metastatic tumors are collected through the Warm Autopsy Program. The Warm Autopsy Program allows University of Pittsburgh HSTB to collect metastatic tumors that might otherwise not be available. It also has institutional review board (IRB) approval to access the medical records of the cancer patients to retrieve medical histories. About 5 percent of the tissue at University of Pittsburgh HSTB comes from clinical trial work. Individuals who are potential tissue sources are recruited in the clinical offices, usually by an oncologist and a research nurse coordinator.

Ardais and GCI collect tissue from surgical patients. Individuals who contribute tissue to Ardais are recruited by research nurses working (typically) within the pre-op admissions area, while GCI tissue sources are recruited by participating physicians or by full-time employees responsible for recruitment and tissue collection at GCI's collection sites. (GCI's Web site also has information for those who are interested in volunteering to donate tissue.)

Minority Populations, Children, and Foreign Tissue Sources

As Table 3.1 shows, all of the repositories collect specimens from minority populations. Some repositories set out to include as much diversity as possible. For example, Philadelphia Familial Breast Cancer Registry has funding to specifically genotype minority families for BRCA1 and BRCA2.[2] CHTN also tries to collect tissue from as broad a spectrum as possible from different racial and ethnic groups, but specimen collection is a function of the requests submitted by researchers. In addition, CHTN divisions reach out to community hospitals to increase the diversity of the specimens collected. Others collect specimens from minorities based on the diversity of the patients/volunteers seen at that institution. For example, the specimens at Duke University Breast SPORE, Mayo Clinic Prostate SPORE, the UAB Breast and Ovarian SPOREs, and University of Pittsburgh HSTB reflect the distribution of minorities seen by those institutions (including any collaborating/contributing institutions). Still others, such as NHLBI LAM Registry and Ardais collect specimens based on defined clinical characteristics, not specific demographic characteristics. Collecting tissue from ethnically diverse populations of all ages in order to ensure diversity of the tissue available for research purposes, to be demographically representative of the population, and to expand biomedical research to include understudied/underrepresented populations and to study health disparities is a **best practice**.

---

[2] Mutations in BRCA1 and BRCA2 (breast cancer 1 and 2 genes) make some people more susceptible to developing breast and other types of cancer. Women who inherit a mutated BRCA1 or BRCA2 gene have an increased risk of developing breast and/or ovarian cancer at a young age (before menopause) and often have multiple close family members with the disease. These women may also have an increased chance of developing colon cancer. Men with a mutated BRCA1 or BRCA2 gene have an increased risk of breast cancer and prostate cancer. Alterations in the BRCA2 gene have also been associated with an increased risk of lymphoma, melanoma, and cancers of the pancreas, gallbladder, bile duct, and stomach.

CHTN, EDRN, University of Pittsburgh HSTB, and AFIP collect specimens from children. For example, CHTN Pediatric Division is dedicated to the procurement of pediatric specimens. In addition, several of the CHTN divisions and University of Pittsburgh HSTB include collection sites at children's hospitals. Ardais has IRB approval to collect specimens from minors using a parental consent process, but it has not started to do so. Philadelphia Familial Breast Cancer Registry would also like to start collecting specimens from children.

Several of the repositories also collect specimens from tissue sources in other countries. AFIP receives tissue specimens from all over the world, TARP has collaborations with investigators that collect specimens from Poland and China, and GCI has (or has had) collection sites in Belgium, Poland, Tunisia, Vietnam, and India. Several of the participating EDRN centers have ongoing collaborations with the United Kingdom, Canada, and Israel. Philadelphia Familial Breast Cancer Registry also collects specimens from family members residing outside the United States, and two of the other breast and ovarian CFRs are located outside the United States, in Canada and Australia.

Collection Locations

For the most part, specimens are collected at academic medical centers and community hospitals. CHTN Eastern Division also works with eye banks and organ procurement organizations to obtain eyes and organs for research use. Specimens sent to AFIP have been collected at hospitals (both academic and community) and private physicians' offices. Philadelphia Familial Breast Cancer Registry also gets blood, collected by family physicians, from participants' family members. Blood for NHLBI is also collected at clinical laboratories, while tissue specimens from individuals with LAM are removed at medical facilities (community hospitals and academic medical centers). As mentioned earlier, specimens at Duke University Breast SPORE, Mayo Clinic Prostate SPORE, the UAB Breast and Ovarian SPOREs, and University of Pittsburgh HSTB come solely from their affiliated academic medical centers. Ardais collects from three academic medical centers and one hospital. GCI has an extensive network of 700 collection sites throughout the United States and in several foreign countries. Establishing a network of collection sites is a **best practice** in an effort to obtain a variety of specimen types and to be demographically representative of the population.

Biospecimen Collection

Most of the repositories/collection sites use some combination of pathologists, pathology assistants, histotechnologists, tissue technicians, and trained repository personnel for the collection of tissue. NHLBI, Duke University Breast SPORE, and Philadelphia Familial Breast Cancer Registry use phlebotomists and clinical personnel to collect blood samples. Researchers are typically not part of the specimen collection process.

A typical scenario for tissue collection at most of the repositories is as follows: Pathology assistants or other trained repository personnel monitor the operating room (OR) schedule to determine when a surgery is going to occur from which tissue will be collected. (Duke University Breast SPORE noted it was no longer able to identify tissue sources through the OR schedule due to HIPAA requirements.) The surgeon removes the tissue according to whatever surgical procedure is performed, and the tissue is sent to the pathology laboratory. A pathologist examines the tissue and takes what is necessary for patient diagnosis and decides what portion of the specimen is excess and can be released to the repository. At several repositories, the patient's diagnosis is rendered by the pathologist before the specimen is given to the repository in order to ensure that the specimen is not needed for further diagnostic workup. Allowing pathologists to determine what tissue is necessary for pathologic diagnosis and what is excess and available to give to the repository for storage and research use is a **best practice.** The portion of the specimen intended for the repository is immediately given to trained repository personnel (usually a pathology assistant or histotechnologist), who begin processing the specimen either for preservation and storage or for immediate shipment if requested fresh.

The number of people employed to collect, process, store, and distribute tissue varies among repositories. Each repository has its own organizational structure and procedures for collecting, processing, and storing tissue, which influence the number and types of personnel utilized to carry out these processes. For example, CHTN, Ardais, and GCI have core personnel at their center of operations who are employees of the repository, and they have additional personnel at the collection sites who are trained by the repository but are employees of the collection site institutions. CHTN also sends its own employees to collection sites in their immediate geographic area. In contrast, all of the personnel involved in repository functions at AFIP are employees of AFIP, but since AFIP is a referral center, it does not have personnel at the collection sites.

The following list gives several examples of the numbers and types of personnel involved in repository functions:

- CHTN Eastern Division has 12 to 13 FTEs (full-time equivalents), including the people assigned to distribute TARP microarrays and to carry out national marketing, but not counting personnel at the satellite sites. CHTN Eastern Division has seven to eight primary staff members and several others with less than full-time commitments (e.g., some pathologists may only dedicate approximately 10 percent of their time to CHTN work). Other staff are distributed among the remote sites, but the amount of their time spent doing CHTN work is approximately equal to two FTEs. At satellite sites, specimens are collected either by CHTN Eastern Division staff from the University of Pennsylvania who go to the site or by CHTN-funded and -trained staff who work at the site. The number of people working at remote sites depends on the needs of researchers requesting tissues from CHTN.
- The collection, storage, processing, and distribution of specimens for EDRN are done at the individual network participant locations, primarily academic medical centers, using standardized protocols.

- AFIP is not involved in the collection of specimens. It employs 75 people to receive, store, maintain, and retrieve the tissue specimens. In addition, ten volunteer high school students work with the repository staff.
- Mayo Clinic Prostate SPORE has six individuals who are trained to collect and process tissue (two at each of the two community hospitals affiliated with the Mayo Clinic and two at the Mayo Clinic, where tissue is stored), and a team of individuals (a registered nurse, a pathologist, and two scientists) that oversees the disbursement of tissue.
- University of Pittsburgh HSTB has one medical director, one laboratory manager, seven tissue bankers, three cancer registrars, two laboratory technicians, two cancer biomarker technicians, and one medical fellow (who assists with data management) working in the tissue bank and affiliated laboratories. There is also a director of Oncology and Pathology Informatics and a director of Research Informatics, as well as a team of bioinformaticians.
- Ardais has six to eight FTEs at each of four collection sites who are employees of the hospitals, but whose salaries, benefits, and overhead are reimbursed by Ardais via a grant mechanism. The typical contingent includes research nurses (informed consent process), multiple part-time pathologists (initial banking decision and management), a pathology assistant (specimen banking SOPs), a histotechnologist/tissue technician, a repository clerk (local repository management/shipping), and clinical data managers. Additionally, the protocol principal investigators (the chair or vice-chair of Pathology) have management responsibilities but are not compensated. Ardais currently has approximately 60 employees and consultants at their headquarters in Lexington, MA.
- GCI has 27 employees at its headquarters in Cambridge, MA. There is also one FTE at each collection site. The GCI people at the collection sites (e.g., community hospitals) are paid by the collection sites, an arrangement the site agrees to when it signs up to be a GCI collection location. Although the site people are

not GCI employees, this arrangement ensures that there is one person at each collection site dedicated to the consent, collection, and shipping of specimens to GCI.

Centralized Versus Decentralized Collection and Storage

There are three main models of collection and storage operations: decentralized collection with centralized storage, centralized collection and storage, and decentralized collection and storage (Figure 6.1, in Chapter Six, provides a diagram of different centralized and decentralized models). Many of the repositories are decentralized in the collection of specimens—meaning there are multiple collection sites that are geographically dispersed, usually involving some combination of academic medical centers and community hospitals—but store their specimens in a centralized facility (TARP, NHLBI, AFIP, Ardais, and GCI). Some repositories have both centralized collection and storage, such as Duke University Breast SPORE, the UAB Breast and Ovarian SPOREs, and Mayo Clinic Prostate SPORE, whose specimens come solely from their affiliated academic medical centers.

In contrast, both collection and storage of specimens are decentralized for CHTN, EDRN, the Breast and Ovarian CFRs (of which the Philadelphia Familial Breast Cancer Registry is a member), and University of Pittsburgh HSTB. Specimens collected by the six CHTN regional divisions and their collaborating community hospital sites are usually transferred to the main regional division sites and distributed from there, while fresh (meaning not frozen) specimens usually go directly from collection sites to the researchers. The specimens collected for EDRN and the CFRs are stored at collection/storage sites that are geographically dispersed. University of Pittsburgh HSTB collects and stores specimens at four academic medical centers that are part of the UPMC hospital system.

When specimens are sent to a centralized storage facility, most are transferred via overnight service (e.g., Federal Express® [FedEx®]) or by local couriers. EDRN, the SPOREs at Duke University and UAB, and University of Pittsburgh HSTB store specimens locally. Mayo Clinic Prostate SPORE collects tissue from two affiliated hospitals that are connected to its processing facility.

Repositories that collect tissue from multiple sites each have their own procedures for shipping specimens to a centralized storage facility—by international shipping companies (e.g., FedEx®) or local couriers, at room temperature, on dry ice, or in liquid nitrogen. All of the repositories follow International Air Transport Association (IATA) regulations for transporting hazardous substances, when applicable. For example:

- At CHTN Eastern Division, specimens procured locally are transported on wet or dry ice by the procuring technician or local courier service. Specimens from non-local collection sites are sent via FedEx® on dry ice. Fresh tissue from all collection sites goes directly to the researcher. Shipments are scheduled, expected, and monitored by CHTN Eastern Division. Tracking of shipments and expected receipts is integrated with the bioinformatics system. Shipping containers and procedures are standardized, training is provided, and CHTN Eastern Division monitors adherence to the standards. All applicable regulations are met or exceeded. Changes in regulations are monitored by the CHTN Regulatory Affairs Subcommittee, participation in the International Society for Biological and Environmental Repositories (ISBER), and guidance from local institutional safety officers.

- Philadelphia Familial Breast Cancer Registry supplies FedEx® kits to remote collection sites for overnight shipment of samples via FedEx®.

- NHLBI ships specimens via courier (FedEx® or private courier) in containers with dry ice. Containers are tested in house both for individual unit function (i.e., temperature probing and mock shipment) and for design quality (e.g., test to failure to determine container limitations). BBI validates that all shippers are using proper configuration and containers. The clinical sites fill out a form to accompany the specimen and send a copy of the form to the Data Coordinating Center (DCC). If something is wrong with the specimen, then it is tracked in the tracking folder. If shippers continually ship incorrectly, BBI cites the transport regulations and refuses to accept specimens if the packages do not meet regulatory standards.

- Ardais ships all of its specimens from the medical centers to Ardais headquarters via FedEx®. Standardized and carefully monitored shipping procedures are integrated with Ardais's information technology system, which tracks all shipments and expected receipts. The specimens are packed in dry ice in self-contained, pressurized containers within an IATA-approved external container.

- GCI provides collection personnel with vapor-shippers for tissue specimens and collection kits for blood and serum specimens. All collection kits are tagged with a bar code label that denotes the specimen collection site. The same bar code is attached to the collection tubes. GCI tissue specimens are shipped in liquid nitrogen vapor-shippers and sent via FedEx®. DNA, plasma, and serum are packed on ice and shipped overnight as they are collected. Blood is also shipped out as it is collected. The bar codes on all the specimens are scanned once they arrive at GCI.

Using standardized and carefully monitored shipping procedures with systems to track all shipments and expected receipts is a **best practice.**

Quality Assurance, Auditing, and Standardization for Biospecimen Collection

Most of the repositories verify the integrity of every tissue after collection: CHTN, TARP, Philadelphia Familial Breast Cancer Registry, Duke University Breast SPORE, Mayo Clinic Prostate SPORE, the UAB Breast and Ovarian SPOREs, University of Pittsburgh HSTB, Ardais, and GCI. Quality assurance (QA) procedures at these repositories include matching the tissue received with the pathology report and other documents provided with it and review by a pathologist of an H&E (hematoxylin and eosin) stained slide made from each specimen. This is a **best practice.** In contrast, some repositories depend on the sites that collect the original specimen. For example, AFIP acquires tissue specimens that have been collected and processed at the institutions that originally obtained the tissue from patients. EDRN requires that QA measures be built into protocols and that the protocols undergo extensive peer review before it approves them.

Some repositories may also perform additional, quality control (QC) testing. For example, material used in the construction of tissue microarrays by TARP may be subjected to additional QC, including RNA integrity by in situ hybridization and immunohistochemical staining to match known profiles. GCI also checks RNA integrity and performs genetic marker tests on blood to verify and characterize the specimens.

Ardais and GCI also utilize a standardized collection protocol, collection kits, and a bar-coding system to track specimens. For example, GCI provides the collection personnel with collection kits for blood and serum samples and vapor-shippers for tissue specimens. All collection kits are tagged with a bar-code label and that same bar code is attached to the collection tubes. Additional bar-code labels are provided in the kit; these are attached to all paperwork associated with that specimen. The specimens are tracked during collection and storage using this bar code. BBI and University of Pittsburgh HSTB also use a bar-code tracking system. Using an electronic tracking system to track specimens and associated information is a **best practice**. Currently, bar codes are used for this purpose, but additional electronic technologies, including smart cards and radio-frequency identification tags, are available.

Many of the repositories have developed SOPs for collection of their specimens: CHTN, TARP, EDRN, Mayo Clinic Prostate SPORE, University of Pittsburgh HSTB, Ardais, and GCI. This is a **best practice**. In addition, CHTN, University of Pittsburgh HSTB, Ardais, and GCI train collection personnel and provide standard protocols for them to follow. This, too, is a **best practice**. CHTN uses a combination of CHTN staff and CHTN-trained personnel who are employees at the collection sites. University of Pittsburgh HSTB uses trained pathology assistants at its collection sites. Ardais and GCI train personnel who are employees at the collection sites.

CHTN, TARP, and Coriell Cell Repositories (CCR), which stores and distributes specimens for Philadelphia Familial Breast Cancer Registry, also monitor the quality of the tissue they distribute through feedback from researchers receiving the tissue. A questionnaire sent to researchers with each shipment asks for feedback on the quality of the tissue that was received. For example, the questionnaire sent by CHTN to researchers with each shipment asks for feedback on everything from the quality of the tissue and the accompanying data that were sent, to the packaging and the timely receipt of the sample. CHTN also sends a more extensive annual questionnaire to researchers that solicits input on past quality, current usage, and future needs. Many of the other repositories also request feedback from researchers, but the process is less formal.

QA processes ensure the integrity of both the clinical and the technical aspects of the operation. QA at participating institutions that provide tissue is assured, for the most part, by pathologists at the repository, who check the quality and verify the diagnosis of the tissue that was sent. In addition, Ardais and GCI scan the bar codes on specimens and check them against the shipping manifest and other paperwork. EDRN's participating centers or laboratories are subject to biennial site visits by NCI personnel and outside advisors, or to more frequent visits if NCI deems they are necessary.

CHTN Eastern Division has daily interactions and is in constant communication with its collection sites through phone calls and e-mail. This level of communication is integral to CHTN Eastern Division's ability to fill researcher requests and identify needs or problems at collection sites. University of Pittsburgh HSTB and Ardais also ensure standards at contributing institutions through weekly contact with medical center site personnel and monthly operations meetings/phone conferences. Ensuring standards at institutions that contribute specimens to the repository through close contact with collection site personnel is a **best practice**.

Some of the repositories require that certain standards be met by institutions that provide tissue. For example, EDRN participants are required to adhere to principles laid out by EDRN. Each proposal to EDRN undergoes extensive peer review before being approved. To remain in the network, EDRN participants must reapply for funding every five years, at which time they must verify that they are following EDRN standards and protocols. In contrast, TARP, Philadelphia Familial Breast Cancer Registry, NHLBI LAM Registry, and AFIP accept some specimens "as is" from submitting institutions and evaluate the quality of a specimen after it arrives at the repository.

GCI has taken action against several DNA and tissue collection sites that lacked appropriate QA standards. TARP will also drop collaborators that chronically submit poor-quality specimens. Ardais communicates lapses in standardization or quality back to collection sites and addresses them during co-management activities. Major lapses could result in termination of a banking agreement between Ardais and an institution as a collection site, but such action has not taken place to date.

Biospecimen Processing and Annotation

Careful and well-documented processing and extensive annotation of tissue specimens are crucial to the overall usefulness of the repository as a resource for scientific research. Although it is important and necessary to remain flexible in meeting researcher needs in order to keep pace with new approaches in biospecimen research, a certain level of standardization will always be needed for such research to be applicable and useful in the long term. Some of the repositories evaluated for this study stress the standardization of all their specimens, while others focus on remaining flexible to be able to respond to as many different researcher requests as possible. Details about biospecimen processing and annotation at the repositories evaluated are provided in the following subsections.

Biospecimen Processing

Biospecimen processing procedures can involve the physical treatment of the specimens both at the time of their collection and after their receipt at the repositories. Techniques for processing the actual specimens at collection sites at the time of collection varied across the repositories evaluated. At CHTN, where specimens are collected and treated according to researcher requests, these procedures are not strictly standardized. The processing of specimens at CHTN varies according to the protocol of each individual investigator: (a) fresh tissue can be collected aseptically and sent to researchers in transfer media of their choice, (b) specimens can be snap frozen, or (c) specimens can be fixed or paraffin embedded. While CHTN is able to provide researchers with customized procurement, the basic techniques used to process the specimens are standardized (e.g., snap freezing is done the same way each time, paraffin embedding is done the same way, and time of formalin fixation is the same) unless the researcher specifically requests that the processing be done differently. For instance, CHTN Eastern Division reported that approximately 80 percent of the specimens collected are procured and processed for storage within one hour post-excision, as processing specimens as quickly as possible makes them useful for the broadest possible range of researchers.

The UAB Breast and Ovarian SPOREs try to collect and process some specimens from each case within 15 to 30 minutes of availability in the OR. Additional tissue from the case is often collected in Surgical Pathology. All UAB SPORE specimens are frozen and stored in the vapor phase of liquid nitrogen. All Duke University Breast SPORE specimens are frozen within one hour of extraction and stored in mechanical freezers at −135°C with liquid nitrogen backup. At Mayo Clinic Prostate SPORE, the tissue specimens are sent to a hospital accessioning area after collection, at which point the repository technicians are notified. The specimens are then treated with OCT (optimum cutting temperature) embedding compound, snap frozen, and placed in −70°C freezers. At University of Pittsburgh HSTB, tissue bankers are in constant contact with the OR to minimize the time from when the tissue is excised until it is frozen. Most specimens are collected within one hour of excision and are snap frozen in an isopentane bath unless a researcher requests a different procedure.

BBI, EDRN, and AFIP do not deal directly with collection and initial processing of specimens. EDRN does regulate the processing procedures of its network collection sites in order to standardize the specimens; and, similarly, specimens being stored at BBI are collected according to clients' protocols (in this case, the NHLBI LAM study). AFIP does not require standard collection procedures for the specimens it receives.

Ardais has detailed, standardized protocols for specimen preparation. These protocols are followed uniformly at all collecting sites. All equipment is provided by Ardais and is standard at all locations. Over 70 percent of specimens are collected within one hour. A pathologist immediately reviews each specimen to determine which portion of it is available for use by Ardais. Specimen preparation is customized to the type of tissue being processed. Typically, specimens are cut to provide a reference sample (destined for formalin fixation and paraffin embedding) flanked by one or more samples (destined for freezing). Frozen material is embedded in OCT. The orientation of the specimens is specified such that cutting surfaces reflect adjacency. Samples are part of a "module" with defined structure so that the physical adjacency of every sample from a specimen is maintained in the database. Each sample container is bar coded and logged into the system. Fixation times are controlled and logged into the database for each sample.

GCI also provides collection site personnel with standardized protocols to follow for preparation of specimens for the repository and collection of medical information from donors. The majority of specimens at GCI were procured in less than one hour. The processing of specimens after arrival at GCI varies depending on the sample type (e.g., RNA extraction from tissue, transformation of cell lines from lymphocytes). Procurement and processing of specimens for storage within one hour post-excision using detailed, standardized protocols is a **best practice**.

At Ardais, BBI, and GCI, where regular shipments of specimens are received from collection sites, somewhat similar procedures are followed. Shipping manifests are checked against both a list of expected specimens and the actual contents of the shipment. At Ardais and GCI, this is just a matter of matching the codes on the vials to those on the lists; at BBI, a data collection sheet is filled out for every shipment.

Tissue Characterization and Quality Control Testing of Biospecimens

Several of the repositories perform histopathology (H&E staining) on all tissue specimens, which is reviewed by a pathologist. For example, a CHTN pathologist reviews a QC H&E slide from every specimen collected by CHTN. The pathologist verifies tissue morphology as well as other tissue characteristics, such as percentage of tumor, necrosis, fibrosis, and mucin. In addition to assuring researchers that the tissue they are receiving is really what it is labeled, this approach provides a valuable tool for oversight of the quality of samples from contributing institutions. This is an important adjunct to the oversight provided by the local pathologists at the satellite collection sites, who are charged with overseeing procurement (under CHTN direction) at their own institutions. At TARP, not only is an initial H&E slide evaluated from each paraffin block of tissue chosen for inclusion in an array, but also, once the array is constructed, every 50th slide cut from the tissue microarray is H&E stained and evaluated.

Mayo Clinic Prostate SPORE verifies all tissue by microscopic examination of H&E stained slides. H&Es and other stains are scanned, and the digital images are placed on a server for other researchers using the tissue. This conserves tissue and prevents depletion of tissue that might otherwise be used for repeat H&E slide preparation. At UAB, a paraffin block is made that corresponds to each specimen, and a slide is H&E stained and reviewed by a pathologist. Researchers are provided with information about the specimen found when reviewing the H&E slide. University of Pittsburgh HSTB has a digital whole-slide imaging system that allows pathologists to evaluate samples over the Internet. Ardais uses in-house and consultant pathologists to confirm the pathology reports received with the specimens and verify each specimen. Digital images of specimens are available through a Web-accessible interface prior to distribution to researchers, or to generating tissue arrays or molecular derivatives. GCI has hired two pathologists from nearby Massachusetts General Hospital to review and annotate records based on review of the H&E stained slides. Verification and evaluation by a pathologist of tissue specimens collected by the repository is a **best practice**.

A few of the repositories routinely perform other standard laboratory tests on the specimens upon their arrival. These often involve more extensive clinical characterizations of the specimens. In addition to its H&E slide review procedures (discussed above), TARP performs immunohistochemical tests and in situ hybridization on specimens for QC purposes. GCI performs genetic marker tests on all blood/sera received and follows extensive procedures to standardize the volume and concentration of these specimens. (Specimen identity and characterization are checked and monitored throughout these procedures.) GCI also routinely performs RNA extractions on a subset of its tissue specimens. University of Pittsburgh HSTB also performs RNA integrity checks on a subset of its specimens. When repositories perform these types of tests, any results or further annotation collected are usually provided along with the pathology report that is given to the researcher. At most repositories, however, special tests or preparations (such as DNA, RNA, protein preparations, tissue microarrays, immunohistochemistry, and laser capture microdissection) are done only at researcher request.

Results and annotations gathered from H&E stained slides or any other assays or tests performed on the specimens upon arrival and throughout their lives at the repository are linked to the specimens and provided to researchers, a practice followed to some extent by all repositories evaluated for this study. This procedure is a **best practice**. Providing information about the specimen obtained during the QC histopathologic examination and tissue characterization (including digital images of stained slides, when appropriate) in a database for other researchers to access is also a **best practice**.

Data Collection and Specimen Annotation

Most repositories collect basic pathology data about each specimen, which usually includes demographic and diagnostic information. Some also try to collect medical history and clinical outcomes data

(Table 3.2). For example, the type of data available with most specimens collected by CHTN, NHLBI, AFIP, Duke University SPORE, University of Pittsburgh HSTB, Ardais, and GCI includes the pathology or autopsy report ("scrubbed" to remove all patient identifiers) and basic demographics (age, race, and sex). Ardais provides an abstracted version of the pathology report to its customers using standardized nomenclature. Mayo Clinic Prostate SPORE collects limited patient information with its specimens.

EDRN requires network collection sites to collect certain common data elements (CDEs) with each specimen (a technique also used by the Breast and Ovarian Cancer Family Registries and Ardais). Decisions about what to include as CDEs are made collaboratively by EDRN members; after a new CDE is proposed, there is a brief period during which members may comment on the usefulness or necessity of the new CDE and voice their opinions on whether or how it should be included. Weekly committee discussions are held to address questions that arise regarding the CDEs. A core set of CDEs is collected by EDRN members for every specimen; it includes demographic information, tobacco and smoking history, cancer history, family cancer history, and menstrual history. Additional CDEs are collected that are tailored to the type of specimen being collected (e.g., tissue or blood specimens) and the organ site (e.g., breast, prostate, or colon). Sometimes diagnostic information or information about the patient's medical history is also available. Specimens collected by researchers prior to joining EDRN are often added to the EDRN database. The data accompanying these specimens is translated into the EDRN CDEs using a tool that was developed specifically for this purpose. Once the data on each specimen are collected, they are added to the on-line database that links all of the collection sites participating in EDRN. TARP is also implementing the Tissue Microarray Data Exchange Specification, which is a tool for organizing tissue microarray data in self-describing XML documents using a set of CDEs (Berman, Edgerton, and Friedman, 2003). Ardais has a defined minimal data set for each specimen accrued. When relevant to the diagnosis, those data elements are common across specimens.

Table 3.2
Biospecimen Annotation

Repository	Pathology Data	Clinical Data	Longitudinal Data	Genomic/ Proteomic Data	Other Research Data
CHTN	Yes	Yes (limited cases)	Yes (limited cases)	No	No
TARP	Yes	Limited (only with collaborative studies)	Limited (only in certain collaborative studies)	Yes, only from collaborative studies	Yes, only from collaborative studies
EDRN	Yes	Yes	Yes	No	No (not yet)
Philadelphia Familial Breast Cancer Registry	Yes	Yes	Yes	Yes, UC Irvine Informatics Center	Yes, UC Irvine Informatics Center
NHLBI[a]	Yes	Yes	Yes	No	No
AFIP	Yes	Sometimes	Yes (limited cases)	No	Whatever the submitting pathologist includes
Duke University Breast SPORE	Yes	Yes	Yes	No	Yes

Table 3.2 (continued)

Repository	Pathology Data	Clinical Data	Longitudinal Data	Genomic/ Proteomic Data	Other Research Data
Mayo Clinic Prostate SPORE	Yes	Yes	Yes	No	Limited
UAB Breast and Ovarian SPORE	Yes	Yes	Yes	No	No
University of Pittsburgh HSTB	Yes	Yes	Yes	Yes, from a demonstration project with 100 prostate cancer samples	No
Ardais	Yes	Yes	Yes (just started)	Yes, for specific researcher requests	Working on a clinical genomics database
GCI	Yes	Yes	Yes	Yes, only for samples used for internal/ collaborative research	Yes, only for samples used for internal/ collaborative research

[a]Data are for the NHLBI LAM Registry. No data about the specimen are available at the repository itself. The LAM Registry collects clinical, longitudinal, pathology report, diagnostic, demographic (gender, ethnicity), medical history, family history, medical and surgical treatment, and quality of life data. Survival is an outcomes variable.

Many repositories collect additional information with their specimens beyond that included in the pathology report: CHTN, NHLBI, EDRN, the UAB Breast and Ovarian SPOREs, University of Pittsburgh HSTB, Ardais, and GCI (Table 3.2). For example, at GCI a 10- to 15-page case report, collected with every specimen, includes demographic data, information about the patient's lifestyle, diet, and family history, and some disease-specific information (such as medications, diagnostic methods, and any adverse reactions to medications). For the disease-specific information, GCI follows the nationally accepted "Gold Standard" criteria.[3] Data deemed necessary by the current literature and governing organizations to ensure proper diagnosis are also required and collected by GCI (e.g., specimens collected representing coronary artery disease must include a copy of the angiogram confirming this diagnosis). Survival data are not available for tissue specimens because the links back to the patients are destroyed, but links are maintained to most DNA and serum specimens. For some samples, CHTN also collects information about treatment with chemotherapy or radiation, and about estrogen receptor/progesterone receptor (ER/PR) status for breast cancer samples. EDRN collects, through its CDEs, some medical/family history information, which is available in its searchable databases.

The Breast and Ovarian Cancer Family Registries (and Philadelphia Familial Breast Cancer Registry) was designed to support research on genetic epidemiology, clinical epidemiology, and social and behavioral epidemiology. Therefore, the data it collects are quite different from those collected by most of the other repositories. For example, Philadelphia Familial Breast Cancer Registry collects demographic information, as well as data on family history (covering three generations), medical history, epidemiological history (heavily weighted to reproductive history because the registry deals with breast and ovarian cancers), cancer screening history (e.g., mammograms), smoking/exercise/dietary history, medication use, exposure to radiation and/or chemotherapy, and psychosocial measures. Philadelphia

---

[3] The Gold Standard is a medical diagnostic industry standard.

Familial Breast Cancer Registry also conducts an annual follow-up to get information about changes in health status and cancer screening status.

University of Pittsburgh HSTB has well-annotated patient data, including demographics, medical history, lifestyle information, medication use, and treatment history. University of Pittsburgh HSTB's Organ Specific Database has disease-specific information, including tumor grades, that is generated through its interface with the Cancer Registry.

Best practices for data collection depend on the mission of the repository. Collections of biospecimens used primarily for basic research may only require minimal associated clinical data, such as demographic data and pathology reports, whereas collections used for translational research (e.g., target identification or validation) may require more in-depth associated clinical data, such as medical and family histories, treatment data, and clinical outcomes data. No matter what the requirements for the amount of associated data are, certain best practices are applicable. Collecting consistent and high-quality data associated with biospecimens and employing a standardized set of CDEs that are collected with every biospecimen are **best practices**. In addition to basic demographic and pathologic data, some repositories also collect extensive data on family history, medical history, lifestyle and diet, treatment, and clinical outcomes. Collection of complete data on all elements in a minimal data set designed to fulfill the mission of the repository and meet the needs of its users is a **best practice.**

Longitudinal Data

All of the repositories evaluated for this study collect longitudinal data, but they do so to different extents (Table 3.2). The ability to effectively collect and store longitudinal data is a **best practice.** CHTN collects longitudinal data for limited cases when requested to do so by researchers and the data are available. Longitudinal data are not collected for the TARP microarrays distributed through CHTN, but such data are part of some of TARP's collaborative studies, in which case they are collected by the collaborating researchers. Each repository that collects longitudinal data does so in its own way; for example:

- Philadelphia Familial Breast Cancer Registry collects longitudinal data through an annual questionnaire that is sent to participants. If a patient has had a new diagnosis of breast or ovarian cancer, Philadelphia Familial Breast Cancer Registry also tries to obtain a sample of the tumor.
- The UAB Breast and Ovarian SPOREs track longitudinal data through a tumor registry. At Duke University Breast SPORE, a laboratory technician tracks longitudinal data through on-line medical records and a tumor registry. BBI tracks longitudinal data through a unique identification number given to each specimen. When AFIP gets new tissue from the same patient, it is tracked longitudinally by its unique AFIP identification number, and AFIP may follow up clinically with how a patient is doing.
- At Mayo Clinic Prostate SPORE, the Bioinformatics Department has access to the clinical information through the clinical databases. Information about everyone who comes to the Mayo Clinic for a radical prostatectomy is automatically entered into the database, and pre-operative, operative, and follow-up data are collected. If a patient does not come to Mayo for follow-up visits, he or she is automatically sent a follow-up questionnaire a year later. If the questionnaire is not returned, a letter seeking the information is sent to the referring doctor.
- University of Pittsburgh HSTB tracks longitudinal data through the cancer registry, which automatically updates the repository data system. A case number is assigned for each patient/disease combination (i.e., a patient keeps the same case number if he/she comes back for follow-up visits, but if the patient comes back for a different disease, he or she gets a different case number). Each organ system has a cancer registrar in charge of the database. The cancer registrar performs the clinical annotations using North American Association of Central Cancer Registries

(NAACCR) cancer registration standards and a common data pool.

- Ardais recently started collecting longitudinal data upon request. These data are linked to the specimen via the case identification number. Only the dedicated personnel for data collection at the clinical sites can access the link to patient identifiers. Collection and de-identification of longitudinal data occur solely through those individuals working with Ardais-supplied case report forms.

- GCI collects longitudinal data on approximately 85 percent of blood, serum, and DNA that it collects. It does not obtain longitudinal data on tissue specimens, because these specimens have been unlinked (i.e., the links back to the patients are destroyed), so it is not possible to go back for additional information about the tissue sources. A link is maintained for most DNA and serum specimens, however. GCI uses a third party to keep the forms linking patients to their specimens.

Quality Assurance, Auditing, and Standardization for Processing of Biospecimens

At several repositories, each specimen is subject to a pathology verification process. CHTN Eastern Division utilizes several layers of QA, auditing, and standardization for its processing of biospecimens, including QC checks for histology and pathology that are performed by a CHTN pathologist, and a feedback questionnaire that is included with each shipment to ask about the quality of the samples received. As noted above, TARP stains every 50th slide cut from a tissue microarray block with H&E to check the integrity of the array, and may perform additional immunohistochemistry and in situ hybridization studies to check for quality. Duke University Breast SPORE verifies all tissue before use in research assays by H&E analysis. Mayo Clinic Prostate SPORE examines a frozen section from every tissue collected by H&E staining; it also does this after sections of the tissue have been cut from the specimen to ensure that there is still relevant tissue available for use. At Ardais, this pathology verification process adds a significant number of quantitative and qualitative data fields. Likewise, a slide of every tissue specimen is examined by a pathologist upon arrival at GCI. The pathologist confirms the identity and diagnosis of the specimen and makes further annotations about its characteristics, including any special/unusual attributes. QC checks for histology and pathology by repository pathologists is a **best practice**.

Quality Assurance, Auditing, and Standardization for Annotation of Biospecimens

Laboratory procedures followed by several of the repositories to standardize and verify the actual specimens as they are received was discussed above. Separate procedures are needed to manage and verify the information collected through these various standardization, processing, and annotation processes. For instance, each repository has developed its own way of checking and absorbing into its database information from pathology reports and other medical documentation received with the specimen.

University of Pittsburgh HSTB has developed an integration system that automatically accesses the surgical pathology report, the cancer registry, and the repository database and extracts data into the repository database. For prostate tissue, the integration system also performs an automated de-identification procedure that has been extensively tested to ensure that it can de-identify patient records while entering data into the tissue bank database. University of Pittsburgh HSTB routinely runs queries against the system to find data that are inconsistent, and continually checks the metadata dictionary to update the way data are converted.

As mentioned, Ardais sends abstracted pathology reports with the samples it sends to researchers. This is the result of a series of procedures developed by Ardais to minimize manual data entry at all stages of the tissue banking process. In addition to bar coding all of its sample vials and storage boxes, Ardais hires physicians to continually create and apply a standard terminology to all of its data collection procedures. Raw pathology reports are abstracted using controlled vocabularies into structured data fields with quantitative and comparable values. Additionally, each sample is subject to a pathology verification process, which adds a significant number of quantitative and qualitative data fields. Structured data are required to support both database queries and the computational analysis of experimental results. Structured data also allow the creation of Web-deployed data-entry forms complete with drop-down menus and other features that minimize the errors associated with typing information into forms. CHTN also uses standardized histopathology terminology and drop-down menus to standardize the data in the database.

In a different approach, GCI uses a split screen (scanned-in original document on one side, blank GCI-specific form on the other) to help avoid data-entry errors. The data are entered into the GCI form manually. The scanned version of the original is there should anyone have any questions in the future. Ensuring the accuracy of data entry through the use of standardized terminology and computer data-entry forms (e.g., drop-down menus) whenever possible is a **best practice**.

Another strategy to minimize data-entry error is to include several additional checks in the process. CHTN Eastern Division reported using several checkpoints to make sure that the proper data are attached to the proper specimen. Specimen labeling is checked upon receipt of the specimen into the laboratory to confirm that all label information is correct and that no patient identifiers exist. After data entry, the information is verified by a second party to confirm that data entry is correct. CHTN Eastern Division has also developed a parsing technique, which involves using a computer program to review the text of the pathology report and confirm these data against the data that were entered into the database. The program notifies the user if there is a discrepancy and keeps records of when error tracking and reconciliation are done. Similarly, the GCI bioinformatics system automatically checks for consistency and omissions in the data accompanying the specimens.

Philadelphia Familial Breast Cancer Registry also has edit checks built into its system to look for consistency and data that are out of boundaries. The UCI Informatics Center does more edit checks when the data are sent to the CFRs central bioinformatics system and provides discrepancy reports for each CFRs site on data submission (i.e., it provides a detailed report showing errors case by case). The discrepancy reports are posted to a special secure Web site.

Most repositories conduct at least one independent check of the data once they are entered into a database. Procedures at AFIP call for at least three checks of information sent with specimens to the repositories, one of which is performed by a pathologist. All data at TARP and BBI are double key punched (i.e., data are entered twice), cross-reviewed, and checked.

In the decentralized repositories, such as EDRN, these checks are performed at a higher level. Specifically, EDRN's Data Management and Coordinating Center requires (a) accuracy checks on the data mapping from the collecting institutions to the CDEs (these reviews are performed by two people); (b) validation checks comparing query results of the EDRN database to expected values from the institution's database; and (c) integrity checks that involve standard and random queries used to evaluate results and look for anomalies in the EDRN database. Ardais also reviews data for consistency during its pathology verification process. Implementing one or more independent checks of the data once they are entered into the repository database is a **best practice**.

One additional aspect of QA at repositories is the tracking of specimens in the repository (i.e., anonymization, location, volume, and distribution status). The repositories evaluated revealed similar strategies for addressing these issues. Most repositories reported already using or having definite plans to implement a system to track specimens through scannable bar codes. Such codes are used to track all information about a specimen over its lifetime at the repository. Several repositories mentioned specifically soliciting feedback from researchers regarding the quality and usability of the samples received. At CHTN, if the quality issue is tissue specific, this feedback is reassociated with the portion of the specimen still remaining in the repository. AFIP, which uses a unique seven-digit code for identifying each of its specimens, reported also having standard procedures for dealing with specimens received from patients who already have specimens stored in the repository. When this happens, the specimens are given the same accession number but a new sequence number.

University of Pittsburgh HSTB is also able to track patients through its database. If a patient returns to the health system at UPMC and has additional tissue procured, the database is able to make the identification and link the new information to the previous record.

Biospecimen Storage

Number and Types of Tissue in Storage

The number of tissue specimens stored at the repositories evaluated ranged from 1,100 prostate cancer specimens at Mayo Clinic Prostate SPORE to over 90 million specimens representing the entire spectrum of human disease at AFIP (Table 3.3). The types of stored tissue at all repositories include tissue from several types of cancer, tissue from other diseases, non-diseased matching adjacent tissue (i.e., microscopically uninvolved by disease), blood, serum, plasma, urine, and normal tissue from autopsy, organ donation, or tissues from patients undergoing surgery for an unrelated condition.

More specifically, the Pediatric Division of CHTN stores approximately 85,000 specimens, including cancer, adjacent normal, and benign disease tissue. CHTN's mandate is to distribute specimens, not to store them, although there are always some specimens that are in process and/or banked. TARP usually stores between 500 and 2,000 paraffin blocks of tissue in-house. These paraffin blocks of tissue are received, cores of tissue are removed and used to make the tissue microarray blocks, and then the tissue blocks are returned to their place of origin. Each tissue microarray block contains approximately 300 to 500 cases. TARP usually has between 25 and 50 active array blocks to be cut and approximately 2,000 to 3,000 slides of arrays in storage. TARP collects primarily tumors, with approximately one-quarter having matched normal tissue. EDRN's repositories contain over 382,000 specimens, with a focus on cancer tissues. These tissues have a number of normal and matched disease-specific controls. AFIP houses 2.8 million cases comprising more than 12 million wet tissue specimens, 30 million paraffin-embedded specimens, and

Table 3.3
Biospecimen Collection, Processing, Storage and Distribution

Repository	Number of Tissue Specimens Stored	Number of Tissue Samples Distributed	Number of Investigators Receiving Tissue	Type of Tissue	Tissue Processing
CHTN	Children's Oncology Group: ~85,000; Eastern Division: ~1,000–2,000 frozen tissues; ~10,000 paraffin blocks; ~20,000 slides	>62,000 in FY 2001 (>200,000 samples since 1987; CHTN Eastern Division: ~21,000/yr increasing ~5%/yr)	Total: >1,000 (Eastern Division: 380/yr)	Cancer; matching adjacent; other diseases; organs; eyes; serum/blood; fluids/cytology samples; normal	Fresh; snap frozen; paraffin embedded; slides; touch preps; frozen sections; tissue microarrays (TMAs); and ribbons
TARP	5,000–6,000 blocks (1,000/yr); 2,000–3,000 slides of arrays	1,250 slides/yr	125	Cancer; matching adjacent; normal	Paraffin-embedded TMAs; slides
EDRN	382,600	800	N/A	Cancer; normal	Varies by institution

Table 3.3 (continued)

Repository	Number of Tissue Specimens Stored	Number of Tissue Samples Distributed	Number of Investigators Receiving Tissue	Type of Tissue	Tissue Processing
Philadelphia Familial Breast Cancer Registry[a]	1,530 blood samples	26 DNA	2	Blood; breast and ovarian cancer	Frozen (blood); paraffin embedded (tumors); cell lines; DNA
NHLBI	LAM Registry: 1,500; other NHLBI collections: >3,000,000 bloods and blood components[b]	LAM Registry: 2; other NHLBI collections: ~30,000/yr	LAM Registry: 2	LAM Registry: lung and other LAM-related tissue; other NHLBI collections: blood (serum, plasma, RNA, DNA)	Snap-frozen; OCT frozen; formalin fixed; paraffin embedded
AFIP	30 million paraffin; 50 million glass slides; 12 million wet specimens	2–3 sets externally/yr	AFIP researchers and collaborators; outside researchers: 2–3/yr	Cancer (50%); other diseases (50%); blood; urine and other body fluids	Paraffin embedded; glass slides; wet specimens; some frozen (for research)

Table 3.3 (continued)

Repository	Number of Tissue Specimens Stored	Number of Tissue Samples Distributed	Number of Investigators Receiving Tissue	Type of Tissue	Tissue Processing
Duke University Breast SPORE	N/A	~100 /yr (>1,000; 10,000 slides and blood samples since 1987)	N/A	Breast cancer; some normal tissue; blood; serum	Snap frozen; OCT frozen
Mayo Clinic Prostate SPORE	1,100 prostate	250–300 last year; 102 in TMAs	TMAs—10	Prostate cancer (with blood/plasma and urine) and matching benign	Snap frozen; paraffin embedded
UAB Breast and Ovarian SPOREs	700 breast cancers; 500 ovarian cancers; 1,000 uninvolved breast and 1,000 uninvolved ovarian specimens	~50 total (waiting for resource to "mature" before distributing samples)	UAB investigators; Univ. of California, San Francisco Breast SPORE	Malignant; benign; diseased; matching adjacent; blood; serum; normal	Snap frozen; paraffin embedded

Table 3.3 (continued)

Repository	Number of Tissue Specimens Stored	Number of Tissue Samples Distributed	Number of Investigators Receiving Tissue	Type of Tissue	Tissue Processing
University of Pittsburgh HSTB	1,100 paraffin-embedded prostate cancers with slides and matched frozen tissue (70% have associated blood samples);[c] thousands of frozen specimens of other normal and cancerous tissue	2,500 last year (thousands of samples distributed in previous years)	50 UPMC labs	Cancer and metastatic tumors; matching adjacent; normal; clinical trials (~5%); blood	Snap frozen; paraffin embedded; primary cultures of prostate cancers
Ardais	160,000 from over 10,000 cases; 70,000 slides; several thousand RNA stocks	Expect ~5,000–7,000 distributed in 2003	N/A	60% cancer; 40% other (GI inflammatory, bone/joint, etc.)	Snap frozen; paraffin embedded

Table 3.3 (continued)

Repository	Number of Tissue Specimens Stored	Number of Tissue Samples Distributed	Number of Investigators Receiving Tissue	Type of Tissue	Tissue Processing
GCI	20,000–25,000 (tissue only)	~400 tissue; ~800 serum; ~100 RNA; ~15,000 DNA in the last year	~90	Cancer; other diseases; matching adjacent; normal; serum and DNA (diseased and healthy controls)	Snap frozen; paraffin embedded; sera; DNA

NOTE: N/A = Information not available.

[a] Coriell Cell Repositories serves as the storage facility for specimens from three of the six Breast and Ovarian Cancer Family Registries. In addition to the specimens CCR stores and distributes for the Philadelphia Familial Breast Cancer Registry, it stores 4,777 specimens and has distributed 3,415 samples for the Northern California Cooperative Family Registry, and stores 544 specimens and has distributed 355 samples for the Utah Cooperative Breast Cancer Registry.

[b] Data from the NHLBI Biologic Specimen Repository Web site: http://www.nhlbi.nih.gov/resources/medres/reposit/reposit.htm.

[c] The CPCTR, a network of four main collection sites, of which University of Pittsburgh HSTB is one, has a total of 3,800 paraffin-embedded and 800 frozen specimens of prostate cancer.

50 million glass slides, about half of which are from cancer patients. Some frozen tissue is stored as part of ongoing research. BBI currently stores more than 3 million specimens, including blood and tissue from a variety of NHLBI-sponsored studies.

All of the repositories, except the part of BBI associated with NHLBI, store cancerous tissue. The SPOREs collect specimens of cancers specifically geared toward their area of study (i.e., Duke University Breast SPORE only collects specimens of breast cancer, Mayo Clinic Prostate SPORE only collects specimens of prostate cancers). CHTN, GCI, and Ardais store specimens from numerous types of cancer, including head and neck malignancies, and carcinomas of the lung, gastrointestinal tract, breast, genitourinary system, prostate, kidney, and skin. Philadelphia Familial Breast Cancer Registry collects blood from breast and ovarian cancer patients, individuals at high risk for developing breast or ovarian cancer, and family members, and requests specimens of breast and ovarian cancer from patients. University of Pittsburgh HSTB stores biospecimens that are primarily from cancer patients, including specimens from head and neck, lung, liver, breast, gastrointestinal, prostate, bladder, and gynecological tumors, as well as melanomas, sarcomas, blood products, and urine. It also collects normal tissue through organ donation and metastatic tumors through its Warm Autopsy Program. Specimens stored at Ardais are approximately 60 percent cancer and 40 percent other conditions, such as gastrointestinal inflammatory disease and bone/joint disease. Typically, about 60 percent of the neoplastic/lesional tissue specimens are associated with non-diseased matching adjacent tissue. GCI currently stores 60,000 to 80,000 specimens. Tissue from virtually every organ system in the body is collected, as well as DNA and sera from patients with several conditions, including cancer, asthma, diabetes (Type I and II), osteoarthritis, obesity, and others. CHTN and TARP also store tissues from other diseases, including vascular, diabetes, inflammatory, and metabolic diseases.

In addition to specimens of diseased tissue, all of the repositories, except AFIP, NHLBI, and Philadelphia Familial Breast Cancer Registry, collect non-diseased matching adjacent tissue and normal tissue controls from patients undergoing surgery for a different condition, organ donation, or autopsy. For example, TARP and GCI have normal tissue for the entire human body from patients with diseases other than the target disease. In addition, CHTN, NHLBI, Mayo Clinic Prostate SPORE, GCI, Philadelphia Familial Breast Cancer Registry, and the UAB Breast and Ovarian SPOREs also collect blood and/or serum from some patients. NHLBI stores blood samples at BBI for thirteen different studies on blood safety research, the largest one being the Retroviral Epidemiological Study, which is geared toward blood transfusions. NHLBI also stores both blood and tissue at BBI as part of the LAM Registry. Collecting and storing non-diseased matching adjacent tissue, normal tissue, and blood and/or serum samples for comparison to diseased tissue is a **best practice**.

It is important to note that CHTN and EDRN prospectively collect tissue based on researcher needs. Most of the tissue collected by CHTN is shipped to researchers within four to six weeks of procurement (some specimens may be stored for limited periods of time at ultra-low temperatures before distribution to researchers). In addition, some CHTN divisions may store rare tumors and surplus samples until researchers request them. EDRN's repository design is based on a "just in time" model (i.e., the collection of specimens commences with specific studies to be conducted) and therefore does not entail collecting specimens specifically to bank for future use. Other repositories, such as the LAM Registry, Mayo Clinic Prostate SPORE, and University of Pittsburgh HSTB, collect specimens for both banking purposes and prospectively to meet researcher needs.

Storage Techniques

All of the repositories store some frozen tissues for varying amounts of time. Some repositories store all of their frozen specimens at −80°C in mechanical freezers (AFIP, Mayo Clinic Prostate SPORE, Ardais), some store all of their frozen specimens in liquid nitrogen (Philadelphia Familial Breast Cancer Registry), and others store some frozen specimens at −80°C and some in liquid nitrogen (CHTN, NHLBI, the UAB Breast and Ovarian SPOREs, University of Pittsburgh HSTB, and GCI). Duke University Breast SPORE stores its frozen specimens at −135°C in mechanical freezers that have a liquid nitrogen backup. Most of the repositories also store paraffin-embedded tissue and corresponding slides, and some repositories store fresh tissue, blood, serum, and urine.[4] For the most part, banked specimens are stored indefinitely or until the specimen is used up.

Philadelphia Familial Breast Cancer Registry and NHLBI collect and store primarily blood samples. Blood samples collected by Philadelphia Familial Breast Cancer Registry are stored at Coriell Cell Repositories in liquid nitrogen freezers. Blood samples collected by NHLBI are stored at BBI at −80°C in mechanical freezers. Serum samples at GCI are stored in nitrogen vapor freezers organized by disease type. Once processed, sera and plasma are stored at −80°C or colder. DNA is stored in refrigerators (4°C) and freezers (−20°C) equipped with automated retrieval robots (Thurnall system).

Most of the repositories that collect and store paraffin-embedded tissue store the paraffin blocks at room temperature. For example, AFIP stores paraffin blocks in a temperature-controlled warehouse at 21°C (70°F), and Mayo Clinic Prostate SPORE stores its paraffin-embedded specimens in a separate temperature-controlled facility. TARP uses paraffin-embedded specimens to make tissue microarrays, which are themselves also constructed in paraffin blocks and then sliced (i.e., sectioned) onto individual slides. Currently, TARP stores all of its paraffin blocks at room temperature in "office-like" conditions. BBI stores paraffin-embedded specimens collected by NHLBI both at room temperature and refrigerated at 4°C.

CHTN, AFIP, and TARP also store specimens on glass slides at room temperature. At AFIP, glass slides are stored at room temperature and are on a rotating retrieval system. TARP is also currently storing its slides at room temperature in closed boxes away from light. However, TARP is developing new recommendations for the storage of slides.

There is no standard for storage of slides at this time, and there is an ongoing debate in the pathology literature about loss of antigen

---

[4] GCI did not initially store specimens embedded in paraffin but started to include such specimens in their collection in response to user requests.

recognition over time. Currently, there are several ways to store slides. Older slides were routinely dipped in paraffin to form a "paraffin overcoat." Slides are also stored at room temperature in closed boxes away from light. Newer techniques for slide storage involve storing slides under gaseous nitrogen or under vacuum. TARP is moving toward storing slides that are moved often under vacuum, and slides that are put in storage for an extended period under nitrogen.

CHTN stores thousands of specimens at any one time, which is a small percentage of the approximately 60,000 samples it distributes each year. However, most of the tissue is not stored for long, because it is distributed soon after it is collected. CHTN provides specimens that are fresh, snap frozen in liquid nitrogen, frozen in cryoembedding media such as OCT, touch preps, paraffin blocks, sections on slides, serum, plasma, blood, and urine; preparation is driven by researcher requests. The most common preparation request is for samples to be snap frozen in liquid nitrogen. The demand for paraffin blocks has increased since CHTN was established. The majority of specimens are stored for only a short time after they are collected and before they are distributed to researchers and therefore are stored at –80°C in mechanical freezers, although liquid nitrogen storage may be used if specimens are held for longer periods of time.[5] The Pediatric Division of CHTN collects and banks all available tumor, diseased, and normal tissue from pediatric patients. Some of the pediatric specimens are snap frozen, some are snap frozen in OCT embedding compound, and some are fixed and embedded in paraffin.

Developing standards for storage depending on tissue type and storage condition is a **best practice**. However, there is no consensus on the optimum storage condition for specimens. Storage for frozen specimens ranges from –80°C in mechanical freezers to –150°C in the vapor phase of liquid nitrogen.[6] By reducing specimen tempera-

---

[5] CHTN has received feedback from researchers indicating that as long as samples are snap frozen as quickly as possible in the vapor phase of liquid nitrogen, short-term storage at –80°C is adequate for preserving RNA.

[6] In the past, specimens used to be stored in vials in the liquid phase of nitrogen (–196°C). This caused the seals to break or the plastic vial to crack and, as a consequence, resulted in

tures to below the glass transition temperature of water (−132°C), all metabolic activity comes to a halt (Committee on Germplasm Resources, 1978). Therefore, many think that storage below −132°C provides the best preservation of biospecimen integrity. Paraffin-embedded specimens should be stored under conditions that will protect them from melting or other damage (e.g., by water/humidity or insects).

Freezer Maintenance and Backup

Freezers at all of the repositories are generally connected to central alarm systems with personnel on site 24 hours a day, seven days a week, or monitored by an alarm company. Most repositories/storage facilities also have backup freezers available at all times. Some repositories have their freezers connected to an emergency generator service. CHTN mechanical freezers utilize a carbon-dioxide backup and are connected to emergency power supplies, and Duke University Breast SPORE utilizes a liquid nitrogen backup.

CHTN Eastern Division has maintenance agreements that provide professional periodic maintenance on all freezers. Morning and evening temperature checks are logged; temperatures are also checked, and alarms attended live throughout the day. An automated dialer system is used to contact on-call personnel for after-hours temperature emergencies. The repository also cooperates with University of Pennsylvania Hospital security, which monitors CHTN hallways and calls CHTN staff if there is a problem. Gaskets are cleaned and logged weekly, and the freezers are monitored and recalibrated twice yearly in accordance with National Institute of Standards and Technology (NIST) standards. Backups include carbon dioxide on all freezers, emergency power, backup storage space, and dry ice available at all times. Dual-compressor freezers are used because they keep the temperature more stable during opening and closing of the freezer.

---

damage, contamination, or complete loss of the specimen. To avoid such problems, it is now common practice to store specimens in the vapor phase of liquid nitrogen (Holland et al., 2003).

Coriell Cell Repositories, which is responsible for storage of blood samples collected by Philadelphia Familial Breast Cancer Registry,[7] retains one empty liquid nitrogen freezer and one empty mechanical freezer in the event of a failure. All freezers are alarmed and are on emergency generator service. In addition, there are several redundancies in the system, including three storage locations, empty freezers, and three backup generators (two diesel and one gas).

BBI, which is responsible for storage of blood samples and other specimens collected by NHLBI, has computerized real-time temperature monitoring in every freezer. In addition, manual monitoring is done six days per week, the battery condition is monitored weekly, the vents are vacuumed quarterly, and preventive maintenance is done annually. A "validation" protocol is performed on each freezer annually; it involves a six-point temperature test to ensure optimal freezer operation. Staff are always on call in case of equipment malfunction or failure.[8] Each liquid nitrogen freezer is hooked up to a supply of liquid nitrogen that can be injected as needed. There is also a large tank with backup liquid nitrogen on site. To prevent large temperature variations, the doors on the liquid nitrogen freezers cannot be open for longer than 30 seconds, and only one tray may be removed at a time. Specimens that are transported or worked on outside of the storage freezer are kept on dry ice. There are also two backup generators, one of which is sufficient to provide power to the entire building. The entire facility is monitored at all times by security cameras.

The Mayo Clinic Prostate SPORE freezers are in a special room that is monitored by security cameras, alarms, and locks. There is an emergency contact list available to security and facility management

---

[7] Coriell Cell Repositories collaborates with Philadelphia Familial Breast Cancer Registry at Fox Chase Cancer Center, and serves as a storage facility for blood samples and slides cut from paraffin blocks for Philadelphia Familial Cancer Registry, Northern California Cooperative Family Registry, and Utah Cooperative Breast Cancer Registry.

[8] BBI maintains a list of approximately five people per collection, and not more than one person on that list can be out of town at any given time. There is also a research associate or freezer technician on call at all times for one-week shifts. This person must stay within 30 minutes of either storage building at any given time during his or her shift.

so that if the alarms go off, someone is notified immediately. Extra −70°C freezers are kept operational at all times so that tissue can be moved into them when the primary freezer needs repairs.

University of Pittsburgh HSTB has a computerized monitoring system for its liquid phase nitrogen vessels that records temperatures in real time for each vessel around the clock. Any alarm that is triggered is recorded by the system and alerts the central processing unit of the laboratory, which is manned at all times. Similarly, there is an oxygen-level detection system, which is alarmed and alerts the laboratory in the same fashion. All of the mechanical freezers are connected to an automatic dial-out paging system that cycles through personnel until a response is made. The technician responding can call the dial-up number and get the status of all freezers and can audibly check what is happening in the area where the freezers are located.

Ardais has two different backup generators to take over immediately if there is ever a loss of power. Staff are notified when this happens, and logs are kept. A maintenance contract on the freezers provides service every six months. One freezer is kept empty and maintained at −80°C so that if one of the freezers in use had a mechanical problem, its contents could be moved to the empty freezer. All of GCI's on-site 4°C refrigerators and −20°C, −80°C, and liquid nitrogen freezers are connected to a central alarm system that is monitored at all times by a local alarm company that will notify on-call personnel of temperature fluctuations or power loss. These freezers are also connected to an uninterruptible power-supply system and a natural gas–powered emergency generator. Each of the large freezers equipped with an automated retrieval robot has its own generator. In addition, half of all GCI's sera, plasma, lymphocytes, and cell lines from each tissue source are stored on site, and half are stored in an off-site storage facility in Maryland, where each freezer is monitored by a local alarm company. GCI receives from the off-site storage facility a monthly report on each freezer showing each freezer's temperature trend throughout the month and whether any alarms occurred or adjustments have been made.

Around-the-clock monitoring, weekly maintenance, annual major quality checks of freezers, and freezer backup procedures are

best practices to ensure that specimens are maintained at the necessary temperatures and conditions. Freezer maintenance and backup procedures used by these repositories to ensure specimen integrity are:

- Monitoring a central alarm by on-site personnel or an alarm company at all hours with on-call personnel for after-hours emergencies.
- Connecting freezers to backup generators or a liquid nitrogen backup.
- Establishing maintenance agreements with professional periodic maintenance.
- Developing SOPs for daily/weekly/monthly/yearly maintenance
  - Logging of morning and evening temperature checks
  - Weekly cleaning of gaskets
  - Professional maintenance twice yearly
  - Yearly calibration.
- Maintaining enough empty freezer space to allow for quick transfer of specimens from malfunctioning freezers.
- Using multiple storage sites—either on site (i.e., divided between two or more freezers) or at both on-site and off-site locations.

Quality Control, Auditing, and Standardization for Biospecimen Storage

Quality control, auditing, and standardization during the storage of tissues are well defined at Coriell Cell Repositories (CCR) and BBI, repositories that routinely store large numbers of tissues under collaborative/contractual agreements with institutions collecting tissues. AFIP, which stores over 90 million specimens, has a standard protocol that is followed during the processing and storage of specimens. Ardais and GCI, both of which were specifically designed to collect and store specimens for distribution to customers/researchers, use bar codes to track specimens throughout storage and other operational processes.

CCR, which stores specimens collected by Philadelphia Familial Breast Cancer Registry and other Breast and Ovarian CFRs, employs rigorous standards for storage, including storing specimens in multiple locations, sorting specimens while still submerged in liquid nitrogen to avoid temperature fluctuations, and retaining a portion of the specimen in the original container as a primary identifier. CCR has developed numerous SOPs for freezing and storage of specimens, including freezing a biopsy, assigning frozen ampoules a freeze location and storing the ampoules in their assigned locations, checking sealed glass ampoules for leaks prior to long-term storage in liquid nitrogen, and locating and retrieving ampoules in the liquid nitrogen storage tanks. As part of its ISO9000 certification, CCR performs periodic audits of its inventory to verify the location, identity, and quality of the specimens in storage. CHTN also does annual physical inventories, even though it does not tend to store most specimens for years.

BBI, which stores specimens for NHLBI, has established procedures for the receipt of every kind of specimen. The quality of a specimen is checked and confirmed upon arrival by a research associate. A second research associate confirms the permanent location on forms during inventory. This location is entered into the computer by laboratory personnel and confirmed by a manager. Two sets of independent data are generated and compared to verify that they match before a specimen is committed to inventory. In addition, many of the specimens at BBI are bar coded.[9]

AFIP follows a standard protocol for the processing and storage of each specimen. Specimens arrive in Repository and Research Services and are given a seven-digit AFIP number. Each specimen is checked three times to make sure that the AFIP number and the specimen match. Technicians enter the number and the data into the computer, and a lead technician checks the data and releases it to various departments where the receiving secretary checks that the number and the specimen match.

Three years ago, University of Pittsburgh HSTB performed a year-long audit of its system to make sure that everything was stored where it was supposed to be. Tissue that had been used up, tissue

---

[9] BBI intends to eventually label all specimens with bar codes.

with unreadable labels, and tissue that did not match the computer records were discarded and expunged from the records. University of Pittsburgh HSTB has also recently implemented a bar-coding system.

At Ardais, all specimens and the boxes in which they are stored are bar coded. The bar code is used to track the exact locations of specimens in the freezers. When specimens arrive at Ardais, each specimen and the container are scanned. As specimens are pulled or moved to consolidate boxes, the specimens and the boxes are scanned. In this way, the location of each specimen is always known. The repository is also subject to random audits by Ardais corporate auditors to check that each specimen is accounted for.

GCI employs a system of scannable bar codes to track and manage the specimens in the repository. When the specimens arrive they are checked against information provided by collection sites. Serum and DNA samples undergo a multiple-step process to determine their quality and concentration and to verify their identity, which is usually done by testing certain genetic markers to confirm characteristics, such as sex. If the samples meet these criteria, they undergo additional procedures to standardize their concentrations and volumes. At each point in the process, automatic checks are done to verify the sample's coded identity.

Repositories that store specimens for extended periods of time conduct additional tests on or checks of the specimens after the initial characterization and verification procedures. Often these are performed before the specimen is distributed to researchers. Before tissue is sent to customers, Ardais pathologists perform a verification of each sample via H&E staining to ensure that the sample identity is correct and the sample pathology is consistent with the pathology report from the submitting hospital. All samples are annotated with additional, internally generated pathology data, including digital images, which are available on line. At GCI, new slides are periodically made from existing frozen or paraffin-embedded specimens to check for specimen integrity. University of Pittsburgh HSTB monitors the RNA integrity of its specimens. Periodically auditing, performing inventories, and certifying the location, identity, and quality of specimens is a **best practice**.

Specimen Distribution

The repositories vary greatly in how many tissue samples they distribute every year. The government and industry repositories (EDRN, TARP, CHTN, GCI, Ardais, and NHLBI) distribute significantly more tissue samples than do the repositories associated with academic medical centers (tens of thousands versus hundreds to thousands) (see Table 3.3 for more detail). Since 1987, CHTN has distributed nearly 500,000 specimens to more than 1,000 different researchers, including 49,000 samples in 2002 and 62,000 samples in 2001. Eighty percent of these researchers are in academic or government institutions, the other 20 percent are in industry. TARP distributes 1,250 slides per year through CHTN to 125 researchers, of whom approximately 60 percent are academic, 20 percent NIH, and 20 percent industry. Ardais expects that approximately 5,000 to 7,000 tissue samples will be distributed in 2003 to its partner medical centers, other academic institutes, and biotech and pharmaceutical companies. GCI distributed about 400 tissue samples, 800 serum samples, 100 RNA samples, and 15,000 DNA samples to industry and academic and governmental organizations. Roughly 65 percent of GCI's end-users fell into the industry category.

Over the course of the Duke University repository's life, more than 1,000 tissues and tens of thousands of blood samples and slides have been distributed, averaging approximately 100 samples per year. Eighty percent were distributed to academicians, while 20 percent were distributed to government. There was no distribution to industry. Mayo Clinic Prostate SPORE distributed between 250 and 300 samples in 2002, primarily to researchers at Mayo (90 to 95 percent). About 3 percent of the Mayo Clinic Prostate SPORE samples were distributed to other academic/not-for-profit researchers, and the remaining 2 percent were distributed to researchers in industry. Last year, 1,500 patient samples were supplied by University of Pittsburgh HSTB to University of Pittsburgh researchers (10 to 15 grants), about 10 percent of which were distributed as part of sponsored research agreements with commercial users.

At the other end of the spectrum is the NHLBI LAM study. It has distributed tissue to only two researchers, partly because of the rare nature of the tissue and the goals of the registry. AFIP also distributes very little tissue to outside requesters (two to three requests are approved per year), in part because many requesters are not willing to pay the costs of identifying and preparing the tissues for release. Tissue is shared more often when AFIP staff members are collaborators on protocols.

One of the main reasons for the large differences in the quantities of specimens distributed to external researchers is that specimen distribution practices clearly depend on the mission of the repository. If the mission is clearly defined, and the repository evaluates its ability to meet its goals and is willing to change policies, procedures, and practices when the goals are not being met, then this is sufficient.

Shipment of Samples to Researchers

Most of the repositories use similar procedures to ship samples to researchers and to ship specimens from collection sites to the repository (see subsection entitled Centralized Versus Decentralized Collection and Storage, above). Frozen samples are shipped on dry ice, and paraffin blocks and slides are sent at room temperature via overnight carrier according to IATA shipping regulations. Repositories that provide fresh tissue to researchers, such as CHTN and LAM Registry, ship samples on wet ice or cold packs directly from the collection site where the tissue was obtained.

Shipments to researchers include a shipping manifest, which usually contains a list of sample identification (ID) numbers and descriptions of the samples shipped. At CHTN, procured tissue is assigned to a researcher, and the assignment is verified to confirm that it is an appropriate match. When the shipment is set up, the suitability of the specimen for the researchers' requirements is checked again. At the time shipment is set up, the shipping address and shipping account numbers are verified with the researcher and the database. At the time of shipment to the researcher, labels and pathology reports are verified against the packing list to make sure that all of the information is consistent and correct. Essentially, every step of the process is subject to verification. CHTN and CCR also include a feedback questionnaire in each shipment that asks researchers about the quality of the samples received.

Quality Assurance and Standardization of Biospecimen Collection, Processing, Annotation, Storage, and Distribution

The use of standardized protocols for collection, processing, storage, and distribution of specimens, and common data elements (CDEs) for the annotation of specimens at individual network participant locations makes comparative research across participating institutions possible and is a **best practice**. In addition, QA must be multitiered and fully integrated to be effective. The components of a QA strategy should include:

- Train all personnel who are involved in the collection, processing, annotation, storage, and distribution of tissue.
- Standardize collection, processing, annotation, storage, and distribution protocols to ensure the highest quality samples and comparability of research results.
- Perform appropriate QC testing on each specimen, such as histopatholgy (H&E), immunohistochemistry, testing for DNA/RNA integrity, and other QC testing as appropriate.
- Bar-code specimens and data so that it is easy both to match the specimen with the pathology report and other associated data and to locate the specimen in the storage facility.
- Use researcher feedback about sample quality to re-examine QC procedures.

Best practices for specimen collection, processing, annotation, and distribution clearly depend on the mission of the repository. If the mission is clearly defined, and the repository evaluates its ability to meet its goals and is willing to change its policies, procedures, and practices when those goals are not being met, then this is sufficient.

Using trained personnel and SOPs, maintaining contact within networks, and implementing strict QA and QC measures are critical.

Best Practices

Biospecimen Collection

1. Collect tissue from ethnically diverse populations of all ages to ensure that the tissue available for research purposes is diverse and demographically representative of the population, and to expand biomedical research to include understudied/under-represented populations. Most of the repositories collect tissue from ethnically diverse populations. CHTN, TARP, EDRN, AFIP, and University of Pittsburgh HSTB collect specimens from children. TARP collaborative studies, EDRN, the Philadelphia Familial Breast Cancer Registries, AFIP, and GCI collect specimens from other countries, such as Belgium, Canada, China, India, Israel, Poland, Tunisia, the United Kingdom, and Vietnam (see Table 3.1, above).

2. Build a network of academic medical centers and community hospitals to provide the number of high-quality samples and data needed for research purposes. CHTN, TARP, EDRN, Philadelphia Familial Breast Cancer Registry, AFIP, and GCI have established networks of collection sites for the collection of a wide variety of tissue.

3. To ensure that patient care is not compromised, allow pathologists to determine what tissue is necessary for pathologic diagnosis and what is excess and can be given to the repository for storage and research use. This is done at all of the repositories.

4. Use standardized and carefully monitored shipping procedures with systems to track all shipments and expected receipts. CHTN, NHLBI, Ardais, and GCI carefully monitor shipping procedures.

5. To ensure specimen quality, match the tissue received with the pathology report and other documents provided with it, and

have a pathologist review an H&E stained slide made from each specimen. Most of the repositories verify the integrity of every tissue specimen after collection: CHTN, TARP, Philadelphia Familial Breast Cancer Registry, Duke University Breast SPORE, Mayo Clinic Prostate SPORE, the UAB Breast and Ovarian SPOREs, University of Pittsburgh HSTB, Ardais, and GCI.

6. Use an electronic tracking system, such as scannable bar codes or other, new electronic technologies, to track specimens and associated information from the time of collection through the time of distribution. BBI, Ardais, and GCI use a bar-code tracking system, and University of Pittsburgh HSTB has recently implemented a bar-coding system.

7. Develop standard operating procedures for the repository's collection of specimens to allow experimental comparisons. CHTN, TARP, EDRN, Mayo Clinic Prostate SPORE, the UAB Breast and Ovarian SPOREs, University of Pittsburgh HSTB, Ardais, and GCI have all developed standard protocols for biospecimen collection.

8. Train collection personnel and supply them with standard protocols to follow in order to provide comparable specimens for research purposes. CHTN, the UAB Breast and Ovarian SPOREs, Ardais, and GCI all train repository personnel to collect and process biospecimens.

9. Ensure standards at institutions that contribute specimens to the repository through close contact with collection site personnel. CHTN, University of Pittsburgh HSTB, and Ardais maintain close contact with collection-site personnel. This is also true of TARP, since the specimens used to make the TARP microarrays are collected by CHTN.

Biospecimen Processing and Annotation

10. Procure and process specimens for storage within one hour post-excision using detailed, standardized protocols. CHTN, Duke University Breast SPORE, University of Pittsburgh HSTB, Ardais, and GCI procure and process most specimens for storage

within one hour post-excision. The UAB Breast and Ovarian SPOREs collect some specimens from most patients within one hour post-excision.

11. Utilize pathologists to confirm the identity and diagnosis of bio-specimens collected by the repository and to make further annotations concerning any unusual characteristics to ensure detailed accurate information on all specimens. CHTN, TARP, Philadelphia Familial Breast Cancer Registry, the Duke University Breast SPORE, Mayo Clinic Prostate SPORE, the UAB Breast and Ovarian SPOREs, Ardais, and GCI all do this.

12. Link all results and annotations gathered from H&E stained slides or from any other assays or tests performed on the specimens upon arrival and throughout their life at the repository to the specimens and provide this information to researchers. This practice is followed to some extent by all of the repositories.

13. Provide any information about the specimen obtained during the quality control histopathologic examination and tissue characterization (including digital images of stained slides, when appropriate) in a database for researchers to access. Mayo Clinic Prostate SPORE, University of Pittsburgh HSTB, and Ardais provide information and digital images to researchers in their databases.

14. Collect consistent and high-quality data associated with bio-specimens and employ a standardized set of common data elements that are collected with every biospecimen. The use of common data elements makes comparative research possible across the approximately 40 institutions participating in EDRN and the six institutions participating in the Breast and Ovarian CFRs.

15. Collect complete data on all elements in a minimal data set designed to fulfill the mission of the repository and meet the needs of its users. Philadelphia Familial Breast Cancer Registry, University of Pittsburgh HSTB, Ardais, and GCI collect extensive demographic and pathologic data, family history, medical history, lifestyle and diet history, treatment, and clinical outcomes.

16. Collect and store longitudinal data, following applicable consent requirements. Philadelphia Familial Breast Cancer Registry, EDRN, all of the SPOREs, University of Pittsburgh HSTB, and GCI routinely collect clinical outcomes and longitudinal data about tissue sources. Longitudinal data are collected through annual questionnaires, tumor registries, or directly from medical records. The tissue sources for these resources have consented to this follow-up. All of the repositories collect longitudinal data to varying degrees.

17. Ensure the accuracy of data entry through the use of standardized terminology and computer data-entry forms (e.g., drop-down menus) whenever possible. These practices are used by CHTN, University of Pittsburgh HSTB, Ardais, and GCI.

18. Implement one or more independent checks of the data once they are entered into the repository database. Most of the repositories perform independent checks of data for accuracy and completeness.

Biospecimen Storage and Distribution

19. Collect non-diseased matching adjacent tissue, normal tissue, and blood/serum samples for comparison to diseased tissue. All of the repositories except AFIP, NHLBI, and Philadelphia Familial Breast Cancer Registry collect non-diseased matching adjacent tissue and matching normal tissue controls, and TARP and GCI have normal tissue for the entire human body from patients with diseases other than the target disease.

20. Develop standards for storage depending on tissue type and preservation condition (e.g., snap frozen, paraffin embedded, tissue microarray). This practice exists in several repositories but should be "industrywide." However, there is no consensus on the optimum storage condition for specimens. Storage for frozen specimens ranges from −80°C in mechanical freezers to −150°C in the vapor phase of liquid nitrogen. Many think that storage at lower temperatures helps preserve the integrity of the specimens for long-term storage. Paraffin-embedded specimens should be

stored under conditions that protect them from melting or other damage (e.g., by water/humidity or insects).

21. Monitor specimens around the clock, perform weekly maintenance and annual major quality checks of freezers, and use freezer backup procedures to ensure that specimens are maintained at the necessary temperature and condition. BBI and CCR provide excellent examples of these practices.

22. Use multiple storage sites—either on site (i.e., divided between two or more freezers) or at both on-site and off-site locations. CHTN, CCR, and GCI use multiple storage sites.

23. Periodically audit, inventory, and certify the location, identity, and quality of specimens to maintain the value of the specimens in the repositories. CHTN, CCR, BBI, University of Pittsburgh HSTB, Ardais, and GCI employ auditing and inventory and monitor the quality of their specimens.

Quality Assurance and Standardization of Biospecimen Collection, Storage, Processing, Annotation, and Distribution

24. Use standardized protocols for collection, storage, processing, and distribution of specimens and use common data elements for the annotation of specimens at individual network participant locations in order to make comparative research across participating institutions possible.

25. Ensure multitiered, fully integrated quality assurance, including the following:

- Train all personnel who are involved in the collection, processing, annotation, storage, and distribution of tissue.
- Standardize collection, processing, annotation, storage, and distribution protocols to ensure the highest quality specimens and comparability of research results.
- Perform appropriate quality control testing on each specimen, such as histopatholgy (H&E), immunohistochemistry, testing for DNA/RNA integrity, and other quality control testing as appropriate.

- Bar-scode specimens and data so that it is easy both to match the specimen with the pathology report and other associated data and to locate the specimen in the storage facility.
- Use researcher feedback about sample quality to re-examine quality control procedures.

CHAPTER FOUR

Bioinformatics and Data Management

A critical part of the design of a tissue repository is the bioinformatics and data management system. Bioinformatics is an evolving discipline that has been defined in several ways, but all definitions emphasize the use of computer and statistical methods to understand biological data.[1] Bioinformatics often refers to research involving genomics, the study of the genes and their function in a genome, and proteomics, the study of proteins and their function in the genome.[2]

The RAND interview instrument addressed questions regarding the use of bioinformatics systems at the sites, including standardization of data reporting, data searching and mining capabilities, accessibility of data (for researchers, managers, physicians, patients, and the public), network security, and information technology (IT) personnel. All of the repositories had systems that exhibited data standardization, restricted accessibility to data, and multiple security methods, but few of the repositories were designed to share information broadly or to feed research results back into the database. Specific findings from the interviews are described, along with best practices identified by the RAND research team.

---

[1] http://citeseer.nj.nec.com/504741.html.

[2] http://www.ornl.gov/TechResources/Human_Genome/publicat/primer2001/glossary.html.

Use of Bioinformatics Systems

All of the repositories use their bioinformatics systems as repository inventory management tools for tracking collection, processing, and distribution of tissue specimens (see Table 4.1). Most of the repositories also use their bioinformatics systems as tools to manage pathological and clinical information about the specimens, such as demographic and histopathological information and clinical/outcomes information. At some repositories, immunohistochemistry (IHC) images and research results are also included in the bioinformatics systems (TARP, Mayo Clinic Prostate SPORE, University of Pittsburgh HSTB, and GCI). The CHTN informatics system serves as both a standard repository management tool and a central reference database to allow real-time communication about researcher requests and to help CHTN divisions locate samples researchers need from other divisions. CHTN is in the process of upgrading to a Web-based system. The bioinformatics systems at some repositories are also used to de-identify the specimens (CHTN, University of Pittsburgh HSTB).

The bioinformatics systems range from simple Microsoft Access® databases (Duke University Breast SPORE, the UAB Breast and Ovarian SPOREs), to proprietary systems developed in house (TARP, Philadelphia Familial Breast Cancer Registry, AFIP, Mayo Clinic Prostate SPORE, University of Pittsburgh HSTB, and GCI), to systems developed with the help of contractors (CHTN, EDRN, NHLBI, and Ardais). University of Pittsburgh HSTB and Ardais use an Oracle framework for their bioinformatics databases. Currently, University of Pittsburgh HSTB uses Access® to "manage" the repository. However, it is in the process of converting the Access® tables to an inventory system developed in house that interfaces with its Pathology Software (CoPath) and its organ specific database (OSD), and will report tissue utilization by organ or investigator and allow for specimen tracking and data mining. Ardais uses Business Objects® software as a reporting and data mining tool, and uses Web-deployed interfaces for repository management transactions. Ardais initially

Table 4.1
Bioinformatics and Data Management

Repository	Bioinformatics Use	Access to Data	IHC Images	Genomics/ Proteomics Data	Searchable	Minable	Web-Based
CHTN	Repository and pathological/clinical data management	CHTN staff only	No	No	Yes	No	No
TARP	Repository and pathological/clinical data management; research tool for collaborative studies	Information about TARP array availability is publicly available	Yes	Yes (mostly proteomics)	Yes	Yes (only data for collaborative studies)	Limited
EDRN	Repository and pathological/clinical data management; combine/standardize information from various collection sites[a]	EDRN members and approved non-members	No	No	Yes	Yes	Yes
Philadelphia Familial Breast Cancer Registry	Repository and pathological/clinical data management; research tool	Philadelphia Familial Breast Cancer Registry staff only	No	Yes (mostly BRCA1/BRCA2 genotyping)	Yes	Yes (for data in the CFR database at the informatics center at UCI)	Yes[b]

Table 4.1 (continued)

Repository	Bioinformatics Use	Access to Data	IHC Images	Genomics/ Proteomics Data	Searchable	Minable	Web-Based
NHLBI	BBI—Repository management	BBI staff, and PIs or data managers with approved access	No	No	Yes	Yes	No
AFIP	Repository management; limited clinical data management	AFIP staff only	Yes	No	Yes	Yes	No
Duke University Breast SPORE	Repository and pathological/clinical data management	Duke University Breast SPORE staff only	No	No	Yes	No	No
Mayo Clinic Prostate SPORE	Repository and pathological/clinical data management; research tool	Mayo Clinic Prostate SPORE staff only	Yes	No	Yes	Limited (only clinical database available for mining)	No
UAB Breast and Ovarian SPOREs	Repository and pathological/clinical data management	UAB SPORE staff only	No	No	Yes	No	No
University of Pittsburgh HSTB	Repository and pathological/clinical data management; integrate multiple sites and extract data; research tool	University of Pittsburgh researchers only	Yes	Yes (for 100 cases from University of Pittsburgh)	Yes	Yes	Yes

Table 4.1 (continued)

Repository	Bioinformatics Use	Access to Data	IHC Images	Genomics/ Proteomics Data	Searchable	Minable	Web-Based
Ardais	Repository and pathological/clinical data management	Ardais customers and staff; contributing medical center staff	Yes	No	Yes	Yes	Yes
GCI	Repository and pathological/clinical data management; research tool	GCI staff only	Yes	Yes (for internal and collaborative research)	Yes	Yes	No

[a]The EDRN bioinformatics system is designed to collect research results, but such results have not yet been entered into the system.

[b]The bioinformatics system at the Philadelphia Familial Breast Cancer Family Registry is not Web based. However, the centralized bioinformatics system at the University of California, Irvine (UCI), which is utilized by the Breast and Ovarian CFRs, is Web-based, and the information collected by Philadelphia Familial Breast Cancer Family Registry is downloaded to the UCI system via the Web.

used contractors but found that close interaction between users (researchers, hospital employees, and Ardais staff) and the IT group was required to make the system work well. Ardais has now completely integrated informatics personnel with all operational components of the system—from the medical centers, through internal operations, to distribution. Similarly, GCI and University of Pittsburgh HSTB have IT staff working closely with researchers to develop the systems. In most cases, IT personnel are actually co-located with users. Close ties between the bioinformatics system developers, researchers, data managers, and repository management is a **best practice**. The following repositories exhibit this relationship: CHTN, TARP, EDRN, NHLBI, AFIP, Mayo Clinic Prostate SPORE, University of Pittsburgh HSTB, Ardais, and GCI.

Several repositories use a standardized language to categorize and describe biospecimens and enter data into the bioinformatics system. For instance, AFIP and GCI use the Systematized Nomenclature of Medicine (SNOMED®) coding, and Ardais uses a SNOMED®-based ontology.[3] The cancer registrar for each organ system working with University of Pittsburgh HSTB uses NAACCR standards for clinical annotations to the specimens. The UAB Breast and Ovarian SPOREs found that SNOMED® and NAACCR had redundant diagnoses, so they developed a non-redundant version to use. CHTN uses standard tissue coding developed by CHTN pathologists, which is closely tied to the clinical process flow and is designed to minimize user interpretation. TARP uses standard U.S. pathology nomenclature and alternative names where appropriate. EDRN uses the American Joint Committee on Cancer (AJCC) systems of classification of cancer, NAACCR, and NCI's Metathesaurus, which is based on the National Library of Medicine's Unified Medical Language System Metathesaurus and is supplemented with additional cancer-centric vocabulary. Philadelphia Familial Breast Cancer Registry uses a modified version of the standardized form developed by the registry's Pathology Working Group.

---

[3] It is important to note that SNOMED is a redundant language and does not provide standard data elements.

In addition to using standardized nomenclature, sites have various means of ensuring standardization. At Ardais, the surgical pathology data are abstracted and transferred into the Biomaterials and Information for Genomic Research (BIGR™)[4] system by a trained pathologist using drop-down menus to ensure standard data entry. Ardais pathologists work from printed SOPs providing interpretation rules during the abstraction of the pathology report. Some of the repositories were set up to allow, or are testing the ability of, the medical informatics system located at the collection site to interface with the repository's bioinformatics system (CHTN, EDRN, University of Pittsburgh HSTB, and Ardais). The University of Pittsburgh HSTB system automatically accesses the surgical pathology report, the cancer registry, and the repository database and extracts data for the bioinformatics system. In some cases where the data are entered manually (NHLBI and GCI), two people verify the entry. Using either an automated data extraction system or multiple checks of data entry as well as accepted standard language and drop-down menus in the bioinformatics system is a **best practice**.

Types of Data Contained in Bioinformatics Systems

None of the repositories collect genomics/proteomics data as a primary function. University of Pittsburgh HSTB has performed gene expression analysis by DNA microarray using Affymetrix GeneChips® on 100 prostate tissue samples as part of a pilot study of 200 cases. These results and those from researchers who conduct DNA microarray experiments on other tissue samples distributed from University of Pittsburgh HSTB are entered into the bioinformatics system and are available for all researchers to analyze in "in silico" experiments.[5] University of Pittsburgh HSTB is also part of

---

[4] BIGR™ is the name of the Ardais bioinformatics system.

[5] *In silico* (in or by means of a computer simulation) experiments re-analyze data that have already been collected, as well as combine data sets from different experiments and different

the Pennsylvania Cancer Alliance, a consortium of six medical and cancer research centers in Pennsylvania. Data across the six centers, including DNA microarray data, are being integrated based on the University of Pittsburgh HSTB's bioinformatics model. The Web-based system allows researchers to search across all six centers to find tissue for their projects.

Philadelphia Familial Breast Cancer Registry has a supplemental grant to do some genotyping for BRCA1 and BRCA2 and plans to eventually have everyone in the registry genotyped. At Mayo Clinic Prostate SPORE, tissue samples are used for a variety of purposes, and when a researcher performs DNA or RNA analysis of a sample, the information is added to the bioinformatics system. EDRN is planning to create a data warehouse for genomics/proteomics data. Ardais has a two-year grant from NIST to develop a clinical genomics database using structured data domains to collect clinically relevant information for tissue samples.

Only the Breast and Ovarian CFRs, EDRN, the University of Pittsburgh HSTB genomics project, GCI, and Duke University Breast SPORE currently feed data from research on their samples back into the repository data system. Duke's feedback includes only research performed by the initiator of the repository and others closely associated with it. Results from collaborative validation studies are stored in the EDRN bioinformatics system. GCI stores research and assay results, but that information is only available to internal researchers and collaborators. A **best practice** for bioinformatics systems is feeding standard research results and genomics and proteomics results back into the system for other researchers to access.

Data Accessibility

All of the bioinformatics systems are searchable and many databases are Web based (see Table 4.1). Mayo Clinic Prostate SPORE elected

---

researchers and analyze those new data sets using computer-based simulations and mathematical modeling.

not to use a Web-based system, for data security reasons. In some cases, researchers have access to some data (TARP, EDRN, NHLBI, AFIP, University of Pittsburgh HSTB, and Ardais); but in others, Data Coordinating Centers or other data managers retain sole access (CHTN, Philadelphia Familial Breast Cancer Registry, Duke University Breast SPORE, Mayo Clinic Prostate SPORE, the UAB Breast and Ovarian SPOREs, and GCI). For instance, TARP posts arrays that are available on line, and the database is fully searchable for collaborative studies. The system is similar at Ardais, where the BIGR™ system is searchable by both researchers and staff and provides a unified view of specimens stored at any of the repository sites. Specimens can be searched for using a variety of tissue format, sample finding, and case diagnosis characteristics. In contrast, the Mayo Clinic Prostate SPORE and the CHTN databases cannot be directly searched by researchers. At Mayo, researchers submit questions to the Department of Urology to get approval, and the bioinformatics technicians perform the actual search. At CHTN, staff can query for specific tissues, for statistics about tissues collected, stored, and distributed, and for characteristics about the tissue.

The type of information that is available for searching varies depending on the repository. Almost all of the repository databases include basic pathology data and may also include patient demographics. In some cases, searches can be performed on clinical and outcomes data associated with the specimens.

With the exception of CHTN and Duke University Breast SPORE, the data repositories are set up for data mining (sorting through data to identify patterns and establish relationships), but the data that can be mined are limited to specific sets for each repository. The NHLBI LAM, Ardais, and GCI databases were specifically created to allow data mining and advanced statistical analysis to find useful patterns and relationships. For example, the Ardais bioinformatics system can be mined for quantitative, structured clinical data (e.g., demographics, diagnosis, clinical stage, grade, nodal status, pathology, and sample cellular composition) using both available and modifiable high-level and low-level application programming interfaces (APIs). The University of Pittsburgh HSTB system was designed to allow researchers to combine and analyze data from DNA microarray experiments performed by different scientists.

A bioinformatics system that is searchable and minable via varying levels of Web-based access for different individuals (including repository personnel, researchers, patients, and the public) is a **best practice**. To protect the privacy of the tissue sources, the appropriate level of access for different personnel should be addressed by the IRB or bioethics advisory board.

Bioinformatics System Security

Most of the repositories exercise access control to their data, allowing researchers, physicians, and others access to limited data, such as the number of specimens of a specific type of cancer, while maintaining strict control over the ability to manipulate the data. Several repositories, including CHTN, GCI, and the Mayo Clinic and Duke University SPOREs allow only their staff access to the data. The Ardais system permits both role-based and user-based restrictions to be set by administrators. None of the repositories shares its data publicly.

All of the repositories use both electronic and physical means to protect the data. Because the interviews for this study were conducted primarily with physicians and researchers, RAND did not gather detailed information about the physical and network security. At a minimum, each repository uses firewalls and passwords to prevent unauthorized access. Several network security systems are quite sophisticated and include biometrics, encryption, and intrusion detection systems. Most of the university-based systems are physically housed with the university servers and include all of their security measures. Employing network security systems and access control to ensure that privacy is protected and that the bioinformatics system is secure is a **best practice**.[6]

---

[6] The HIPAA data security standard, which was published February 20, 2003, can be found at 45 C.F.R. Parts 160, 162, and 164 (Volume 68, Number 34).

Quality Control, Auditing, and Standardization for Bioinformatics Systems

Each site uses specific processes to ensure and audit quality and standardize data for entry into its systems. Some of the repositories that inherited specimens or have specimens from older studies conducted before the formal repositories were initiated include non-standard information, but often the value (or potential value) of the specimens has led to the specimens and associated data in the bioinformatics system being maintained. Some of the sites manually double or triple check the data entered into their systems using independent technicians or researchers. The other sites rely on automated software or random or requested checks to validate their data.

Best Practices

1. Maintain close ties between the bioinformatics system developers, the researchers, the data managers, and repository management. The following repositories exhibit this relationship: CHTN, TARP, EDRN, NHLBI, AFIP, Mayo Clinic Prostate SPORE, University of Pittsburgh HSTB, Ardais, and GCI.

2. Use either an automated data extraction system or multiple checks of data entry, accepted standard language, and drop-down menus in the bioinformatics system. CHTN uses standard language and drop-down menus, as well as multiple checks and automated parsing to verify the data entered into its database. NHLBI and GCI perform multiple checks of data entry. AFIP uses SNOMED® coding for its bioinformatics system, and University of Pittsburgh HSTB uses NAACCR coding. University of Pittsburgh HSTB has developed an organ specific database (OSD) integration engine to interface with the tissue bank inventory system that automatically extracts data from the surgical pathology report and the cancer registry. Ardais employs pathologists to abstract the surgical pathology report using printed SOPs that provide interpretation rules and to enter the information into the Ardais

BIGR™ system using drop-down menus to ensure consistency of language.

3. Enter standard research results and genomics and proteomics results into the bioinformatics system for other researchers to access. EDRN stores results from collaborative validation studies in its bioinformatics system. The University of Pittsburgh HSTB OSD integration engine includes results from in-house and other researchers' DNA microarray experiments. GCI includes results of assays in its database, but the GCI database is only accessible for internal research and to collaborators. Duke University Breast SPORE feeds back some research results into its database, but only from researchers closely affiliated with the repository.

4. Develop and use a bioinformatics system that is searchable and minable using varying levels of Web-based access for different individuals (including repository personnel, researchers, patients, and the public). The EDRN database is searchable and minable on line through the EDRN secure site, which is available to all EDRN members and those who request special permission. The NHLBI database is designed for data mining, but only by the data coordinating center. Some parts of the University of Pittsburgh HSTB inventory system are accessible over the Web and are minable. This system is available to researchers requesting tissue and is the model for a statewide system of data sharing among six cancer research sites in Pennsylvania. Ardais developed a Web-based interface for its BIGR™ system that has multiple levels of access and is minable and available to researchers and staff. The bioinformatics system at GCI was specifically designed to be minable.

5. Employ network security systems and access control to ensure that privacy is protected and that the bioinformatics system is secure. All of the repositories use both electronic and physical means to protect the data.

CHAPTER FIVE

Consumer/User Needs

Ensuring that a repository meets its user needs involves continual self-assessment and re-evaluation. Repository users in the academic, government, and industry sectors may have different needs or impose different kinds of demands on their repositories. It is important, therefore, to analyze each repository in terms of its initial design and intent as well as its actual customer profile and demonstrated effectiveness.

Customer Profile

Academic, Government, and Industry Users

The consumers of biospecimen repositories include academia, government, and industry. In general, the commercial repositories—Ardais and GCI—sent a higher percentage of their biospecimens to industry than did the academic centers (see Table 5.1). GCI's mission is to conduct collaborative research internally using in-house and other (primarily academic) laboratories. A subset of GCI's banked specimens is, therefore, used for this purpose (see discussion below). GCI reported distributing approximately 400 tissue samples in the past year (a moderate number compared to that of the other repositories evaluated). In comparison, Ardais expects to have distributed between 5,000 and 7,000 samples by the end of 2003 (see Chapter Three, Table 3.3). At University of Pittsburgh HSTB, which

Table 5.1
Consumer/User Needs

| Repository | Consumers/ Users | | | International Users | Distributed Within Institution |
	Academia	Govern- ment	Industry		
CHTN	── 80% ──		20%	Canada	n/a[b]
CHTN Eastern Division	── 68% ──		32%	Canada	n/a[b]
TARP	60%	20%	20%	Canada	n/a[b]
EDRN	Most	0	Some	No	Most[c]
Philadelphia Familial Breast Cancer Registry	~99%	<1%	0	Yes	Most[c]
NHLBI	── 100% ──		0	New Zealand	n/a
AFIP	n/a[a]	n/a[a]	n/a[a]	Yes	Most
Duke University Breast SPORE	80%	20%	0	No	~50%
Mayo Clinic Prostate SPORE	98%	0	2%	Yes	>90%
UAB Breast and Ovarian SPOREs	90%	0	10%	Yes (~10%)	~70%
University of Pittsburgh HSTB	90%	0	10%	No	>90%
Ardais	── 20% ──		60% bio- tech; 20% pharma	Europe	~20%
GCI	── 35% ──		65%	Yes	15%

NOTE: n/a = not applicable
[a]AFIP has not distributed enough tissue in the last five years to make quantifying percentages of researcher affiliation meaningful.
[b]CHTN and TARP do supply tissue to researchers at some of the collecting centers, but all must apply via CHTN.
[c]EDRN and Philadelphia Familial Breast Cancer Registry distribute most of their samples within their member institutions.

reported distributing 2,500 samples last year, less than 10 percent of those samples were distributed to industry users as part of sponsored research agreements. These industry partnerships are focused on specific research projects, and the actual research is often conducted by UPMC researchers. Among the non-commercial repositories evaluated, NHLBI LAM Registry and Philadelphia Familial Breast Cancer Registry distributed samples almost exclusively to academic researchers (100 percent and ~99 percent, respectively), although both repositories have distributed fewer than 30 samples. Approximately 30,000 samples per year are distributed from other NHLBI collections to primarily academic and government researchers. AFIP's samples are distributed only to academic and government users. CHTN, which distributed more than 62,000 samples in 2001, reported that 80 percent of its samples went to academic and/or government users. (CHTN Eastern Division distributed 32 percent of its samples to industry, slightly more than CHTN as a whole.)

Distribution of Samples Outside the Institution
Several of the repositories evaluated conduct or support internal research using samples stored at their facilities. Two of the academic-based repositories (Mayo Clinic Prostate SPORE and University of Pittsburgh HSTB) distribute the majority of their tissue (>90 percent) within the collecting university. Duke University Breast SPORE distributes ~50 percent of its tissue outside the university (see Table 5.1). The UAB Breast and Ovarian SPOREs are in the process of building their inventory and allowing the specimens to "mature" (i.e., keeping the specimens in storage for three to four years to allow adequate time for the collection of clinical outcomes and longitudinal data) and are not currently distributing many specimens. Their goal, when they start distributing, is to distribute at least 30 percent of the tissue outside UAB. Among the non-academic repositories, GCI conducts the most internal research with its specimens. The repository was designed primarily to facilitate collaborative research that uses human biospecimens, and GCI runs the fee-for-service side of the company (i.e., distributing biospecimen samples for use in research) to support its research endeavors. No exact figures were obtained re-

garding the proportion of samples distributed to internal researchers or collaborators at GCI.

Unlike GCI, Ardais does not conduct internal research on its specimens apart from that used to develop new customer services. The question of internal versus external use of samples for research does not apply to places such as CHTN or EDRN, where samples are not kept at any one location or for any particular institution. Any researcher who is a part of EDRN may access samples from any of the networked repositories.

Meeting Researcher Needs

CHTN, TARP, the UAB Breast and Ovarian SPOREs, University of Pittsburgh HSTB, Ardais, and GCI all set some goals for tissue collection or are trying to keep their stocks replenished to keep up with customer demand. CHTN primarily collects tissue prospectively to distribute to researchers based on their requests. CHTN routinely solicits feedback from researchers who use the repository to assess whether their needs are being met. A subcommittee of the coordinating committee reviews difficult researcher requests and tries to find novel methods for obtaining such specimens. CHTN is continually establishing relationships with new collection sites and looking for ways to increase the types of tissue that are in short supply. Some specimens are collected and stored in anticipation of demand, including rare specimens, excess specimens not needed immediately, and specimens from pediatric patients. Likewise, the EDRN repository is designed based on a "just in time" model and therefore does not collect specimens specifically to bank for future use.

TARP attempts to keep an adequate supply of specimens of the tissue types that are in constant demand, such as breast, ovarian, and prostate cancer. TARP has a goal of maintaining between 75 and 100 different specimens each of breast, ovarian, colon, and prostate cancers. The greatest challenge is obtaining enough prostate cancer specimens, because they are in high demand and the amount of tissue removed is very small. TARP is actively expanding its renal cell carcinoma and pancreatic cancer collections, two of the most requested but frequently unavailable tumors. It does not currently have adequate numbers of these two types. Of the top 20 most common cancers, TARP has access to tissues from 16.

The UAB Breast and Ovarian SPOREs are actively trying to collect many specimens (e.g., 2,000 to 3,000 specimens of breast cancer) to have enough heterogeneity (variety) in tumor types, patient medical histories, and clinical outcomes. In addition, UAB wants to enrich its collection with more specimens from minority populations and unusual subtypes of breast and ovarian cancer.

University of Pittsburgh HSTB has targeted, organ-focused collections of all resected tumors from consented patients in the areas of brain, breast, head and neck, lung, melanoma, pancreas, pediatric tumors, and prostate through NIH-funded research programs. In addition, University of Pittsburgh HSTB has IRB approval to collect all resections from all tissue that comes into the surgical pathology department that would otherwise be discarded. Currently, University of Pittsburgh HSTB's supply far exceeds the demand for tissue.

Ardais attempts to keep an adequate supply of specimens to keep up with customer/researcher demand but does not set an exact number of specimens it needs to collect. If more or less of a particular type of specimen is needed, this is communicated monthly to the staff at the collection sites, in particular to the nurses who contact the patients. Goals are set and detailed forecasting is performed to determine if these goals will be met. Regular reports are generated detailing numbers and types of tissue samples distributed to customers and collected from medical institutes so that collection priorities can be quickly changed to match customer demand.

Assessing the needs of researchers, tracking the numbers and types of tissue samples distributed, and using this information to quickly change collection priorities to match customer demand is a **best practice**. For instance, CHTN actively adapts to researcher needs in a variety of ways to ensure it collects the types of tissue needed. Ardais also adapts to researcher requests monthly using reporting and modeling. Likewise, GCI collects tissue specimens daily to keep its stock of tissue replenished. A quarterly assessment of user requests is performed so that target levels can be constantly adjusted.

Review and Prioritization of Requests for Tissue

The review and prioritization systems for tissue requests at academic and commercial repositories have similarities, while those at government repositories are somewhat different. There seem to be four general approaches: (1) first come, first served; (2) priority to members of the network, collaborators, and/or contributors to the repository; (3) prioritization based on merit review of research proposals; and (4) prioritization based on a set policy of the repository. The commercial repositories evaluated distribute tissue on a first come, first served basis. However, researchers at institutions that are collection sites for these commercial repositories receive some level of priority for tissue distribution over other researchers. For instance, at Ardais, 10 to 20 percent of collected tissue is reserved for researchers from the submitting institution. At GCI the system is not as formalized, although researchers at institutions that are involved in the collection of specimens are given a slight priority. Likewise, some academic repositories give priority to researchers at their institutions over other researchers. For example, members of the UAB Breast and Ovarian SPOREs get first priority over SPORE members at other institutions and non-SPORE researchers. University of Pittsburgh researchers whose grants support the collection of tissue for the HSTB have priority over others. In this way, the needs of researchers at collecting institutions are supported by the tissue collection effort, which ultimately leads to more support for the resource and higher investment in the quality of the specimens collected—a policy that is considered a **best practice**.

At CHTN and TARP,[1] samples are provided according to CHTN's priority policy as follows: (1) first priority is assigned to peer-reviewed funded researchers, including researchers from federal and national laboratories; (2) second priority is assigned to developmental and new researchers and to researchers developing new projects in academic centers or non-profit research institutions; and (3) third priority is assigned to other researchers, including those associ-

---

[1] TARP samples are distributed by CHTN Eastern Division and are therefore subject to the same prioritization system for distribution.

ated with for-profit research institutions. Each CHTN division is allowed some discretion in determining special exemptions to the priority policy. Researchers at EDRN laboratories and centers have priority over other researchers for the tissues collected by EDRN, but all requests are subject to a seven-point criteria review by a prioritization subcommittee. This review takes into account scientific merit, study design, technical parameters (e.g., reproducibility, sensitivity, specificity, throughput, automation, and cost), clinical or scientific impact, portfolio balance with EDRN, practicality and feasibility (e.g., amount of tissue, and number of samples required), and collaborative strength. Similarly, the UAB Breast and Ovarian SPOREs give priority to SPORE members at their institutions, then to SPORE members at other institutions, and finally to other researchers whose projects merit the special use of the specimens and data collected by the SPOREs. The Breast and Ovarian Cancer Registries, of which Philadelphia Familial Breast Cancer Registry is a member, collaboratively share their resources with researchers based on the merit of the researchers' proposals.

At most academic and some government repositories, researchers making large tissue requests or requests for rare tissue must first get approval from a biospecimen committee. Mayo Clinic Prostate SPORE refers all large requests to its SPORE Biospecimen Group, which then prioritizes all the requests (in contrast to small requests, which are handled by the pathologist or RN who heads the repository). At University of Pittsburgh HSTB, the process is similar, with large requests going to a tissue utilization committee that is specific to the type of tissue requested and made up of, among others, physicians, researchers, and administrators. The portion of Ardais's repository that is restricted for use only by the donating medical centers is subject to merit review by internal committees. The use of a tissue utilization committee to prioritize tissue distribution based on merit review of all research proposals using standardized criteria, and to ensure equitable distribution of tissue is a **best practice**.

In most cases, the procedure for prioritizing requests for rare or precious tissue is the same as that used for easily available tissue. CHTN, NHLBI, Ardais, and Mayo Clinic Prostate SPORE also mentioned specific policies for regulating the distribution of the last sample of a particular specimen or for limiting the control of an entire specimen or type of specimen by a single researcher. These types of "last file" or single-user policies are a **best practice**.

Unmet User Needs

Meeting user needs may require different approaches depending on a repository's design, customer profile, and product offerings. At a repository like CHTN, where specimens are collected in response to specific researcher requests, unmet user needs generally fall into one of three categories: (1) impossible requests, such as those for extremely large amounts of tissue; (2) impossible constraints, such as requests for tissue collected under unreasonable conditions; or (3) requests for extremely rare tissue. In general these challenges existed at all the repositories evaluated. CHTN Eastern Division voiced related concerns, citing the trend toward early detection of cancers and the use of new technologies that allow for less invasive or more targeted tumor removal procedures, which results in an overall decrease in the availability of cancer tissue. These challenges differ depending on the specialization of the repository itself. For instance, TARP noted specific unmet demands for kidney, head and neck, brain, and pediatric tissue. The more specialized repository at Duke University Breast SPORE rarely received requests that it was unable to fill. Researchers are attempting to work around the problem of decreasing tissue availability by developing new research techniques. For instance, a surgeon at Duke University has developed a new procedure to extract tissue from small lumpectomies because these specimens leave significantly less breast tissue available for banking. Further technical advances will be needed to collect tissue in quantities that meet the needs of researchers.

AFIP, University of Pittsburgh HSTB, Ardais, and GCI all noted the lack of specific technological capabilities or specimen types as their major unmet user needs. At AFIP, the vast majority of the specimens are embedded in paraffin or mounted on slides and therefore not usable for studies requiring fresh or fresh-frozen tissue. University of Pittsburgh HSTB reports that there has been an unmet demand for biological fluid samples and envisions a need to develop a system to track follow-up blood work done on individuals who have donated tissue to the repository. Ardais noted an increasing demand from its customers for more specialized processing and testing of tissue samples before distribution, and more requests for new types of tissue not yet stored in the repository (e.g., aqueous tumor samples, cartilage, and post-mortem specimens). At GCI there is a demand for a serum biomarker platform.

Tracking the Use of Biospecimens

Types of Research/Use of Samples

Some of the repositories provide samples to researchers primarily for basic research (e.g., CHTN and TARP), other repositories provide samples primarily for familial studies (e.g., Philadelphia Familial Breast Cancer Registry) or epidemiological research (e.g., NHLBI), and still others provide samples primarily for translational research (e.g., all of the SPOREs and University of Pittsburgh HSTB) or drug discovery (e.g., Ardais and GCI). All of the repositories have supplied tissue to researchers conducting DNA, RNA, and protein-based experiments. They also all report subsets of the following: fluorescent in situ hybridization, tissue microarrays, immunohistochemistry, gene mapping, pharmacogenomics, cancer biomarker studies, translational research, cell model development, and epidemiological studies. Samples from several of the repositories, including CHTN, TARP, EDRN, Philadelphia Familial Breast Cancer Registry, Duke University Breast SPORE, Mayo Clinic Prostate SPORE, the UAB Breast and Ovarian SPOREs, and University of Pittsburgh HSTB, are primarily used for cancer research.

Metrics and Feedback on Repository Use

Most repositories have in place methods to measure or track how researchers are using their resources. CHTN closely monitors researcher service through its extensive database, often on a daily basis, which allows close integration of supply and demand, and prepares annual reports about the use of the repository. CHTN also evaluates its resource using metrics approved by the NCI Executive Committee, including tracking the number of publications based on research using the tissue resource, devising impact measures, and analyzing the types of research being conducted using the resource. Multiple subcommittees are responsible for evaluating the resource, including the Marketing, Development, and Operations Subcommittee, the Strategic Planning Subcommittee, and the Quality Assurance Subcommittee. CHTN and the Philadelphia Familial Breast Cancer Registry both send postcards with every shipment to solicit feedback on the quality of the samples, the associated data, and shipping. CHTN also sends questionnaires to researchers annually that, in addition to asking questions regarding the quality of samples received, solicits input on current usage and future needs to allow the resource to evolve. Ardais and GCI also solicit feedback directly from researchers, and recipients of GCI samples are encouraged to return for GCI review any samples that fail. Ardais also has such a "return" policy. The effectiveness of the TARP resource is also evaluated through consumer input and direct contact with users. TARP also evaluates itself through comparisons to other commercial vendors providing tissue microarrays. Solicitation of direct researcher feedback on specific samples received allows for more targeted identification of specific problems or inconsistencies among the specimens in the repository and is a **best practice**.

EDRN has taken a slightly different approach. It formed a network consulting committee to assist in the continual re-evaluation of its network's overall concept, mission, and design. The committee monitors the growth of the network and functions as a liaison between EDRN and the greater cancer community. Similarly, University of Pittsburgh HSTB uses tissue bank utilization committees ("organ specific") to measure its usefulness through direct feedback from surgeons, oncologists, pathologists, and researchers. Although not formally a committee, the Mayo Clinic Prostate SPORE holds monthly meetings with scientists on both the tissue collection and the consumer side to discuss issues related to repository tissues. Ardais relies on internal customer service and medical center alliance groups to ensure that researcher feedback is incorporated into collection protocols. In addition, Ardais rigorously analyzes the collection versus distribution metrics of the repository against diagnosis, sample type, tissue type, format, and other characteristics. Evaluation of repository usefulness through committees or review groups in which both providers and users are able to provide input is a **best practice**.

CHTN, TARP, Ardais, and GCI actively adapt to researcher needs in a variety of ways to make sure they are collecting the types of tissue needed. These repositories regularly assess the needs of researchers and track the numbers and types of tissue samples distributed. This information is then used to quickly change collection priorities to match customer demand. Assessing the needs of researchers, tracking the numbers and types of tissue samples distributed, and using this information to quickly change collection priorities to match customer demand are **best practices**.

Best Practices

1. Give priority to researchers at collecting institutions to increase support for the resource and investment in the quality of the specimens collected. All of the SPOREs evaluated and Ardais and GCI reward the efforts of their collecting institutions and offer them at least a slight priority when distributing samples.
2. Use a tissue utilization committee to prioritize tissue distribution based on merit review of all research proposals using standardized criteria to ensure equitable distribution of tissue to as broad a base of researchers as possible. Committees are usually made up of physicians, administrators, and researchers. EDRN, Philadelphia Familial Breast Cancer Registry, AFIP, Mayo Clinic Prostate

SPORE, and University of Pittsburgh HSTB all conduct such reviews.

3. Implement a policy to control the distribution of the last sample of a particular specimen and prevent the monopolization of an entire specimen or type of specimen by one researcher. Such policies help to ensure that samples are available to a larger group of researchers. NHLBI uses a "last file policy" to control the distribution of the last sample of a particular specimen and to alert study personnel of potential depletions in specimen collections. Mayo Clinic Prostate SPORE and Ardais have implemented policies to prevent the control of an entire specimen or type of specimen by one researcher. CHTN has policies to ensure that samples are available to the largest number of researchers, as well.

4. Solicit feedback from researchers on the samples they receive to identify specific problems, inconsistencies, or shortcomings of specimens in the repository or specimens being collected in a certain way or from a certain collection site. CHTN and Philadelphia Familial Breast Cancer Registry both send postcards with sample shipments to researchers to ask for such feedback. TARP, Ardais, and GCI all have policies in place to solicit and integrate direct feedback from researchers.

5. Use committees or review groups composed of both providers and consumers to provide input on the usefulness of the repository resources and evaluate how well the repository is meeting user needs. EDRN, University of Pittsburgh HSTB, Mayo Clinic Prostate SPORE, and Ardais all have formed and use such groups.

6. Assess the needs of researchers, track the numbers and types of tissue samples distributed, and use this information to quickly change collection priorities to match customer demand. CHTN, TARP, Ardais, and GCI actively adapt to researcher needs to make sure they are collecting the types of tissue needed.

CHAPTER SIX

Business Plan and Operations

RAND evaluated twelve repositories, which were grouped into three general sectors: government, academia, and industry (see Chapter Two, Table 2.1). The first category, government, includes two repositories funded by and operated by federal agencies, one repository contracted by a federal agency, and three repositories funded through cooperative agreements with a federal agency. The second category, academia, includes repositories at three major academic medical centers that are funded through Specialized Center Grants (P50s) from NCI, and one repository at a major academic medical center that houses both NCI-funded resources and institute-funded programs. The third category, industry, includes two private companies that operate biospecimen repositories. Different business models are represented within each category, including tissue banking versus prospective collection and distribution, networks versus individual sites, and centralized versus decentralized collection, storage, and bioinformatics systems.

Government Repositories

Six of the repositories evaluated for this study were categorized as government repositories. TARP and AFIP are government-sponsored and government-operated resources. CHTN, EDRN, and Philadelphia Familial Breast Cancer Registry are funded through Cooperative Agreements with NCI. NHLBI contracted out the operation of its Biological Specimen Repository to BBI-Biotech Research Laboratories, a private company. CHTN and EDRN have a small core staff of government employees who facilitate coordination within the respective networks.

Of the government repositories evaluated, all but one were established primarily for the purpose of research. AFIP is foremost a diagnostic referral center and secondarily a tissue bank. AFIP does not seek out specimens for collection and banking; it is sent specimens, unsolicited, from pathologists for diagnostic purposes. AFIP serves as a referral center for pathologists in need of a secondary expert opinion. After AFIP renders a diagnosis, the specimen is stored in its repository (some specimens are returned to the submitting institution upon request). Although its primary function is in the area of diagnosis, AFIP pathologists do conduct some epidemiological research, particularly in clinical pathological correlations.

Academic Repositories

The academic repositories included in this evaluation were all partially government sponsored, usually with funding through a variety of granting mechanisms. All of the academic repositories operate one or more of the SPOREs. In addition to its Breast SPORE, Duke University has a Brain SPORE. Mayo Clinic has a Prostate SPORE, and also collects breast, ovary, intestine, pancreas, heart, brain, skin, bone, kidney, and bladder tissue. In addition to its Breast and Ovarian SPOREs, UAB has a Brain SPORE and a new Pancreas SPORE, is one of the Biomarker Validation Laboratories for EDRN, and serves as the Southern Division of CHTN. UPMC has a Lung SPORE and is also participating in CPCTR and EDRN.

The SPOREs are funded through Specialized Center Grants (P50s) from NCI. University of Pittsburgh HSTB receives most of its funding from NIH, NCI, the Department of Defense, and the State of Pennsylvania. In addition, small amounts of funding are provided by sponsored corporate relationships. A small part of the funding for the biospecimen repositories at Duke University and the Mayo Clinic also comes from private sources.

Industry Repositories

RAND evaluated two industry repositories, Ardais and GCI. Ardais operates as a tissue bank and distribution service. GCI has a dual business model. It operates a fee-for-service tissue bank and distribution center that works primarily with the pharmaceutical industry to collect specimens for drug development, and it also participates in collaborative research with pharmaceutical and biotech companies and academic and government institutions. Collaborations with academic medical centers and government institutions are done on a non-profit basis. GCI and Ardais are privately funded, although Ardais has some public grant money for research projects.

Repository/Collection Site Relationships

How repositories arrange for the collection of specimens varies depending upon the business model. All of the academic repositories collect specimens almost exclusively from their on-site and associated medical facilities; hence, no formal agreements are necessary. The Mayo Clinic Prostate SPORE has gone outside of its hospital system to obtain specimens on rare occasions if there is a specific need that cannot be met otherwise.

The remainder of repositories tend to draw from a mix of community hospitals and academic medical centers for the bulk of their collection. Many of the regional divisions of CHTN have agreements with several community hospitals to enable them to provide researchers with a broad range of samples. For example, the Eastern Division has agreements with several sites to collect specimens, including six community hospitals, two eye banks, and an organ procurement organization. The collection model at Ardais has been designed to be flexible in size, scalable, and deployable at multiple sites. Ardais currently has arrangements with three academic medical centers (Duke University, Beth Israel, University of Chicago) and one hospital (Maine Medical Center) that serve as collection sites. GCI has over 700 collection sites in the United States, and has collected specimens from sites in Belgium, Poland, Tunisia, Vietnam, and India. GCI has made arrangements at the institutional level as well as with individual doctors through its Physician Network™.

The contractual agreements between collection sites and repositories are negotiated on a case-by-case basis. One repository may have different agreements with different collection sites. CHTN has negotiated agreements with some collection sites that provide some funding up front and then reimbursement for certain services or milestones. It also has fee-for-service agreements with some of its sites. GCI reimburses collection sites on a cost basis.

Repository Operations

CHTN, EDRN, the Breast and Ovarian CFRs, and NHLBI all have a coordinating body that oversees the general operations of the repositories and sets procedures and policies. GCI and Ardais have scientific advisory boards. A CHTN coordinating committee consisting of an NCI representative plus two representatives from each CHTN division sets the general operating procedures and policies for the network. Procedures are designed to enhance throughput rather than storage, since the CHTN was not designed for banking. A quality assurance subcommittee sets general standards for the pathology procedures and has developed a procedure manual that is used at all CHTN sites. Issues of quality control are discussed on a continuing basis, and criteria are modified as necessary. In addition, CHTN continually assesses researcher needs for services such as laser capture micro-dissection (LCMD) and tissue microarrays and adds new services when sufficient demand exists. CHTN has other subcommittees, including a marketing, development, and operations subcommittee, a quality assurance subcommittee, and a strategic planning subcommittee.

EDRN has a steering committee that coordinates the work of the consortium and provides major scientific management oversight. It is made up of the network's principal investigators and NCI staff and is responsible for developing and implementing protocols, designs, and operations.

The Breast and Ovarian CFRs, of which Philadelphia Familial Breast Cancer Registry is a member, has a steering committee, which is its official governing body. The steering committee is responsible for developing the core protocols for biospecimen collection, the core instruments for the collection of epidemiological and clinical data, and policy and procedures. The Breast and Ovarian CFRs also has an advisory board, which is an independent, multidisciplinary panel of senior cancer researchers that evaluates requests from researchers for use of the CFRs' resources. The advisory committee makes recommendations on research priorities to the steering committee, which ratifies the recommendations, based on the feasibility of providing the requested resources. The Breast and Ovarian CFRs also has a publications working group that oversees all issues associated with publications.

NHLBI has a DCC. The DCC for the LAM Registry performs its daily operations based on direction provided by its steering committee, data and safety monitoring board, and the NHLBI program office. In addition, a tissue repository committee provides direction to the DCC in regard to biological specimen distribution.

Lessons Learned

Many of those interviewed indicated that when discussions with a medical facility about becoming a participating collection site first begin, it is most productive to talk to pathologists and surgeons rather than administrators. That is, it is important to have "buy-in" up front from the people who will be directly working with the repository. It is also important to have someone involved from the beginning that understands every aspect of the process. Ultimately, it is necessary to establish good working relationships with all levels of collection site staff.

CHTN Eastern Division suggested caution when setting up collections from institutions that are already collecting tissue for other repositories—not only because of competition for specimens, but to minimize redundancy resulting from a specimen from one tissue source being divided up between different repositories. Researchers may unknowingly receive redundant samples if they have submitted requests to multiple repositories.

BBI, which operates the NHLBI repository, suggested that it is important for the repository to be involved in the design phase of a research effort. Storage experts can help determine the best procedures to use and can be helpful in identifying correct equipment, proper shipping techniques, and labeling.

Good communication between the repository and collection site was also considered vital. At CHTN Eastern Division, collection site personnel function as an extension of CHTN staff and are integrated into repository processes. There are contractual requirements for monitoring, reporting, and interaction, and there is often daily contact between CHTN and collection site staff. Ardais staff are in continuous contact with collection site staff, and formal meetings are held on a regular basis. GCI has one full-time staff member whose sole responsibility is to communicate with collection sites. Establishing and maintaining close working relationships with surgeons, pathologists, nurses, and other relevant staff at the collection sites is a **best practice**.

Repository Model

Banking Versus Prospective Collection

Most of the repositories evaluated did both prospective collecting of specimens and banking of specimens. Philadelphia Familial Breast Cancer Registry, NHLBI, AFIP, and the UAB Breast and Ovarian SPOREs are only involved in banking. Both of the industry repositories, Ardais and GCI, are primarily involved in banking but have done some prospective collecting. CHTN primarily conducts prospective collection and distribution of biospecimens and does limited banking. This prospective procurement model enables CHTN to closely tailor specimen preparation to individual researcher requests and needs. Combining banking to collect and maintain a ready supply of tissue with prospective collection to meet researcher needs is a **best practice**.

Centralized Versus Decentralized

CHTN, EDRN, the Breast and Ovarian CFRs (of which the Philadelphia Familial Breast Cancer Registry is a member), and University of Pittsburgh HSTB are decentralized resources deployed through a distributed physical network of geographically dispersed tissue centers that are coordinated and supported by a centralized bioinformatics and data management system networked across the country (see Figure 6.1, A). Their specimens are stored at geographically dispersed sites. CHTN has six regional divisions, located at academic medical centers that collect specimens at those centers and from satellite sites that include community hospitals, eye banks, and organ procurement organizations. Specimens are stored for short periods of time (usually four to six weeks) at each regional site until they are distributed to researchers. The data and information regarding these specimens are maintained in a centrally located bioinformatics and data management system that is accessible by members of the repository network. Each collection/storage site also maintains its own bioinformatics and data management system that links to the centralized system. The bioinformatics systems for CHTN, EDRN, and University of Pittsburgh HSTB are only accessible by repository personnel. Members of the Breast and Ovarian CRFs can upload data to the bioinformatics system, but only staff at the Informatics Center at the University of California, Irvine, have access to download information.

NHLBI, AFIP, Ardais, and GCI have a decentralized collection model but maintain their storage and distribution of specimens and their bioinformatics system at one physical location (Figure 6.1, B).

Figure 6.1
Centralized and Decentralized Repository Models

A. Decentralized Collection and Storage with Centralized Bioinformatics/Data Management

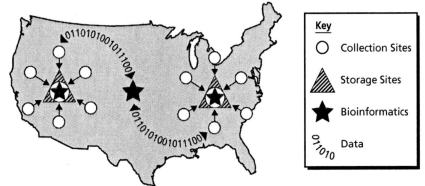

B. Decentralized Collection with Centralized Storage and Bioinformatics/Data Management

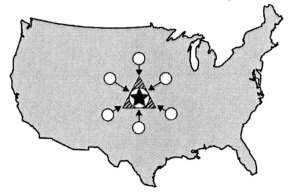

C. Centralized Collection, Storage, and Bioinformatics/Data Management

TARP also has a decentralized collection model with the bioinformatics system and storage maintained at one physical location, but it sends its tissue microarrays to CHTN Eastern Division for distribution to users. Duke University Breast SPORE, Mayo Clinic Prostate SPORE, and the UAB Breast and Ovarian SPOREs have centralized collection, storage, and bioinformatics systems and data management (Figure 6.1, C). These centralized bioinformatics systems have various levels of access. For example, Ardais's system is directly accessible by its customers, but the bioinformatics systems at all of the SPOREs and at GCI are accessible by repository personnel only.

Costs

Repository Costs

Most of those interviewed did not know the cost per sample for their repository to collect, process, store, and distribute tissue. CHTN estimates that it costs approximately $60 per sample shipped. This includes costs involved in collecting, processing, storing, and distributing each specimen. TARP also estimates that it costs $60 to produce and distribute each slide from a tissue microarray. The UAB Breast and Ovarian SPOREs estimate that it costs between $120 and $150 for tissue and data collection per patient, and has an annual operating budget of $80,000 to $100,000 to cover tissue collection and research services. The annual budget for the repository at AFIP is $3.2 million. Likewise, University of Pittsburgh HSTB estimates that it currently receives $2 to $3 million annually either directly or indirectly through grants, sponsored research agreements, and foundation/institutional support for its tissue bank and related informatics program. Ardais collects detailed activity-based costing information for all cases and samples accrued but declined to share that information publicly. GCI also declined to share this information. In many cases, the cost of running the repository was not well known, because the costs are split among multiple grants covering different portions of various personnel's salaries.

Costs to Researchers

CHTN charges academic researchers $20 per sample and charges commercial researchers $60 per sample for the initial processing of the tissue (e.g., snap frozen, paraffin embedded). CHTN uses itemized pricing based on the level of work involved, adding a surcharge for tissue processing in addition to the initial processing (e.g., an H&E slide costs an additional $7, an unstained slide costs an additional $5, and a touch preparation costs an additional $4.50). CHTN is attempting to recover its tissue processing costs. TARP, also moving toward cost recovery, charges academic researchers $40 per slide (TARP first must buy its specimens from CHTN for $20, and then CHTN charges $20 per array for distribution). TARP charges commercial researchers $120 per slide. Tissue microarrays produced by commercial businesses can cost $150 to $200 per slide for 80 to 100 cancer samples, whereas TARP arrays contain smaller cores and a much higher density of tissue samples (300 to 500 cancers).

Philadelphia Familial Breast Cancer Registry charges $1 per microgram of DNA. AFIP attempts to recover some of the processing charges. For example, it charges $2.50 per H&E slide. Other types of tissue processing at AFIP can be as much as $200 a slide depending upon the complexity of the request.

University of Pittsburgh HSTB provides researchers at the university with a small amount of tissue for pilot projects with the understanding that grant proposals will include money in the budget for the repository. There are currently approximately ten to fifteen grants that support the repository's activities. CPCTR, of which Pittsburgh is one of four participating locations, has a set fee structure: $40 per set of samples (four standard 5-micron or two 10-micron slides), $50 for RNA or DNA analysis, and $100 for a frozen tissue specimen not to exceed 0.2 gram. Additional slides cost $3 for a standard 5-micron slide; $4 for 3- to 4-micron slides; $5 for 10-micron slides; $10 for an 11- to 24-micron thick section on a slide; $20 for a 25-micron or thicker section (placed in a tube for polymerase chain reaction [PCR] analysis); and $4 for a slide with an H&E stained section. All charges are tripled for commercial researchers requesting material.

EDRN, NHLBI, and Duke University Breast SPORE provide samples free of charge. Mayo Clinic Prostate SPORE samples are free, although there is a nominal cutting fee if the researcher wants the laboratory to make sections. Samples from the UAB Breast and Ovarian SPOREs are free to members of the SPORE at UAB and are $50 (plus shipping) to all external researchers, both SPORE and non-SPORE members.

GCI negotiates the price per slide under each contract, although standard fees apply. The company declined to give its exact pricing schedule. On research collaborations with academic or government scientists, samples are provided at or near cost or sometimes for free. Ardais declined to publicly disclose pricing but does provide its partner medical center researchers with samples at cost or less.

Although not often practiced, accurate determination of the actual costs of collecting, processing, storing, and distributing tissue samples combined with operating on a cost recovery basis (at least for the government and non-profit organizations) to financially sustain the repository is a **best practice**.

Developing and Adopting New Technologies

All the repositories evaluated claimed to constantly watch for new technologies to improve their processes. Some have regular meetings with staff to brainstorm the issue; others have more formal mechanisms, such as committees or workshops established to purposefully scan for improvements and new technologies.

Some of the repositories are actually involved in creating new technologies and techniques. TARP, for example, develops and promotes new tissue fixation and processing techniques. Duke University Breast SPORE developed a new surgical protocol to collect breast tissue because of increased difficulty obtaining sizable amounts of tissue given more focused breast surgeries. It developed a method of extracting a core from limited resection (e.g., lumpectomy) specimens without affecting the diagnostic ability of surgical pathologists.

University of Pittsburgh HSTB is developing technologies to improve the lifetime of specimens in storage. It has also developed a whole-slide imaging system that takes digital images of whole slides, compresses the files (10:1), and shares them over the Internet, allowing pathologists to evaluate samples without actually having the slide or microscope in front of them. Ardais developed new tissue handling and extraction methods that it supplies to the collection sites.

Continually assessing new technologies and creating a process flexible enough to develop and incorporate added-value technologies into the repository is a **best practice**.

Tracking of Sample Use

The majority of repositories track the number of samples distributed through their bioinformatics system.

Acknowledgments in Publications

All repositories request acknowledgment if their resource is used in research, although few have actual requirements or any form of enforcement. At the academic-based and commercial repositories, no acknowledgment is required, although someone from the repository often is listed as a co-author on the publication. Other forms of acknowledgment include mention in the methods section of the publication or in the acknowledgments section at the end of the publication. Most of the government repositories (CHTN, TARP, EDRN, the Cancer Family Registries, and AFIP) have stricter rules on acknowledgement. In each case, researchers must agree to the acknowledgment in order to receive specimens, and specific wording is suggested. For example, CHTN requires researchers to sign an Agreement for Use of Tissue to obtain samples, and part of that agreement suggests that a specifically worded acknowledgment be used in any resulting publication. EDRN requires acknowledgment and strictly checks for it when collaborators are up for review. AFIP provides a standard disclosure statement, which is detailed in AFIP

Regulation 360-1, "Publication or Oral Presentation of Papers of a Scientific, Technical, or Professional Nature."

Requiring specific acknowledgment of the repository and providing researchers with the specific language to use in publications is a **best practice** because it raises the visibility of the resource and may encourage future participation in and use of the resource.

Best Practices

1. Establish and maintain close working relationships with surgeons, pathologists, nurses, and other relevant staff at the collection sites. CHTN, Ardais, and GCI make concerted efforts to establish and maintain close working relationships with collection site staff.
2. Combine banking to collect and maintain a ready supply of tissue with prospective collection to meet researcher needs. CHTN, Duke University Breast SPORE, Mayo Clinic Prostate SPORE, and University of Pittsburgh HSTB are engaged in a combination of banking and prospective collection.
3. Accurately determine the actual costs of collecting, processing, storing, and distributing tissue samples to researchers, and operate on a cost recovery basis to financially sustain the repository. CHTN, TARP, AFIP, UAB, and University of Pittsburgh HSTB provided information about costs.
4. Continually assess new technologies and take measures to develop and incorporate new technologies into the repository. All the repositories evaluated are constantly evaluating new technologies to improve their processes.
5. Require acknowledgment of the repository and provide researchers specific language to use in publications to raise the visibility of the resource and encourage future participation in and use of the resource. Acknowledgment is required and specific wording is suggested by CHTN, TARP, EDRN, the CFRs, and AFIP. The remainder of the repositories request acknowledgment if their resource was used but do not require it.

CHAPTER SEVEN

Privacy, Ethical Concerns, and Consent Issues

A major concern with the storage and distribution of biospecimens is protecting the privacy of individuals who contribute specimens to the repository and maintaining the confidentiality of the associated data. Another issue is ensuring that these individuals are treated ethically. There are several layers of oversight of research involving human participants, including federal regulations governing research with human participants (the Federal Policy for the Protection of Human Subjects (45 C.F.R. §46; the Common Rule); and the FDA Protection of Human Subjects Regulations (Title 21 C.F.R. Part 50 and Part 56)), state legislation governing the privacy of and research use of medical records, and the HIPAA Standards for Privacy of Individually Identifiable Health Information (Privacy Rule) protecting individually identifiable health information and limiting the ways in which the information can be used. IRB review and informed consent provide additional protections to research participants.

All of the repositories evaluated place great importance on protecting privacy, maintaining confidentiality, and ensuring the ethical treatment of tissue sources. How they deal with these issues varies among repositories and is discussed in this chapter.

Identifiability of Tissue

Two of the questions that were addressed in the interviews regarded how personally identifying information is collected, stored, and distributed along with the biospecimens. The character of the personal information associated with biospecimens as they exist in repositories and in the hands of researchers is based on the schema developed by the National Bioethics Advisory Commission (NBAC, 1999). NBAC determined that biospecimens at repositories are of two types: identified and unidentified. An identified specimen is one that is linked to personal information in such a way that the person from whom the material was obtained could be identified by name, patient number, or clear family relationship. An unidentified specimen is one for which identifiable information was not collected or, if collected, was not maintained and cannot be retrieved by the repository. When the samples are distributed, they may be identified, coded, unlinked, or unidentified. Samples that are coded are supplied by repositories to researchers from identified tissues with a code rather than with any personally identifying information. The researchers do not have access to identifying information, but the sample code can be linked back to the patient by the person or organization that holds the key to the code (e.g., repository personnel, cancer registrar, or honest broker[1]). Finally, unlinked samples (sometimes called *anonymized*) lack any code or identifying information that could be traced back to the original specimen source.

The HIPAA Privacy Rule defines de-identified health information as "health information that does not identify an individual and with respect to which there is no reasonable basis to believe that the information can be used to identify an individual is not individually identifiable health information" (45 C.F.R. § 164.514(a)-(c)). Protected health information can be de-identified by using either this privacy rule's safe harbor method for de-identification or statistical verification of de-identification. Under the safe harbor method, 18

---

[1] An honest broker is a neutral intermediary between the individual whose tissue and data are being studied and the researcher. The honest broker collects and collates pertinent information regarding the tissue source, replaces identifiers with a code, and releases only coded information to researchers. (See the discussion below, in the subsection entitled Protection of Privacy and Confidentiality, for more discussion on the use of honest brokers.)

identifiers[2] that could be used to identify the individual or the individual's relatives, employers, or household members are removed from each record, and the remaining information cannot be used, alone or in combination with other information, to identify the individual. Using NBAC's schema, coded and unlinked samples would be distributed to researchers with de-identified protected health information. Another approach is to use a "limited data set" with a data use agreement. A limited data set allows repositories to provide dates and limited geographic information, but most of the HIPAA identifiers are still removed.

All repositories evaluated for this study collect some, if not all, specimens with identifying information (see Table 7.1). In most cases the identifying information is kept in a database that is linked by codes and accessible to very few personnel, and in many cases it never reaches the actual repository where the specimens are eventually stored. GCI is an exception in that the link between the tissue specimens collected and the tissue sources' identities is permanently destroyed after 30 days by a third-party contractor.

Ardais, like GCI, does not receive identifying information with the specimens it receives from the collection sites; therefore, the specimens are stored as unidentified. In both cases identifying information is collected from the tissue sources, but the link between the tissue sources and the information never reaches the repository. For all blood/sera collected for GCI, the document linking the tissue source's identity with the specimen code is sent to a third-party contractor after the 30-day period. Similar to GCI's treatment of blood/sera, Ardais keeps all information linking the tissue source's identity to the specimen at the collecting institutions.

BBI, which stores specimens for NHLBI, also does not receive identifying information or any link between identifying information and the specimen regardless of whether this information was initially

---

[2] The identifiers that must be removed include direct identifiers, such as name, social security number, medical record number, health plan beneficiary number, street address, telephone/fax number, e-mail address, vehicle license plate number, as well as other identifiers, such as birth date, admission and discharge dates, date of death, and five-digit zip code.

Table 7.1
Identifiability of Tissue

Repository	Identifiability of Specimens in Repository	Identifiability of Specimens Distributed to Researchers	When and Where Samples Are De-identified
CHTN	Unidentified; identified	Unidentified; unlinked; coded	Unidentified/unlinked/coded at collection sites before sent to CHTN, or at CHTN after data collection is complete
TARP	Unidentified	Unidentified	Receives unidentified tissue samples
EDRN	Identified	Coded	Coded at each participating institution
Philadelphia Familial Breast Cancer Registry	Identified	Coded	Coded at FCCC before being sent to CCR for storage
NHLBI	Unidentified	Unlinked; coded	Unlinked/coded at collection sites before being sent to BBI; codes are maintained by the DCC
AFIP	Identified	Unlinked; coded; identified	Coded when they arrive at AFIP, unlinked when they are released to researchers
Duke University Breast SPORE	Identified	Unlinked	Coded at repository after collection; unlinked before distribution
UAB Breast and Ovarian SPOREs	Identified	Coded	Coded at repository after collection
Mayo Clinic Prostate SPORE	Identified	Unlinked; coded	Unlinked/coded at the repository after collection
University of Pittsburgh HSTB	Identified	Unlinked; coded	Unlinked/coded automatically by bioinformatics system when data are extracted from records
Ardais	Identified; unidentified	Coded	Coded at collection sites before being sent to Ardais
GCI	Unidentified (tissues); identified (blood/ sera/ DNA)	Unidentified; unlinked; coded	Unidentified/unlinked/coded at collection sites before being sent to GCI

collected. NHLBI has a tissue repository committee that oversees the security of patient data. TARP does not receive any identifying information with the tissue samples it gets from CHTN; however, some of the samples it receives from collaborators may be identified.

CHTN, EDRN, Philadelphia Familial Breast Cancer Registry, AFIP, the SPOREs, and University of Pittsburgh HSTB all store identified tissue specimens. Identifying information is kept with the specimens at AFIP and EDRN, although this information is not available in the database. CHTN Eastern Division receives identified specimens collected at the University of Pennsylvania Health System, but specimens from other satellite sites are sent to CHTN unidentified. This is also true of other CHTN divisions. Identifying information is kept in the database at Duke University Breast SPORE, but access to this information is limited to two people. At Mayo Clinic Prostate SPORE, all specimens are stripped of identifying information and given a unique ID number. Identifying information on each tissue source can still be linked to the specimens if the appropriate consent is obtained. At University of Pittsburgh HSTB, specimens are identified, but only a few repository personnel, trained as honest brokers, have access to the identifying information.

All repositories except TARP and Duke University Breast SPORE distribute coded samples (see Table 7.1). CHTN mostly distributes coded samples, except for those that come from satellite collection sites and from Vanderbilt, which are unlinked. All information distributed with the samples is de-identified. AFIP distributes coded and unlinked samples, with any links to personally identifying information kept at the repository. AFIP also distributes some identified samples, but only if researchers have the appropriate IRB approval and the need for informed consent has been waived by the IRB. NHLBI noted that if personal information were required by an investigator, the repository (BBI) would not be involved in the process and the request would instead go solely through its DCC. At GCI, all tissue samples are distributed as unlinked samples (i.e., the link is destroyed after collection), whereas blood, serum, and DNA samples can be distributed as coded samples. In contrast, the TARP tissue microarrays are distributed only as unidentified samples, and Duke University Breast SPORE distributes only unlinked samples.

Institutional Review Boards

IRBs are responsible for the oversight and review of research that involves human participants to ensure that their privacy is protected and confidentiality of data is maintained. In 1997, the Office for Human Research Protections (OHRP) issued guidance for human biospecimen repositories sponsored by the Department of Health and Human Services (DHHS):

> Operation of the Repository and its data management center should be subject to oversight by an Institutional Review Board (IRB). The IRB should review and approve a protocol specifying the conditions under which data and specimens may be accepted and shared, and ensuring adequate provisions to protect the privacy of subjects and maintain the confidentiality of data. The IRB should also review and approve a specimen collection protocol and informed consent document for distribution to tissue collectors and their local IRBs. A Certificate of Confidentiality should be obtained to protect confidentiality of repository specimens and data. (OHRP, 1997)

Therefore, the collection, storage, and distribution practices of federally funded repositories, as well as the research for which the investigator is requesting tissue samples, may be subject to IRB review and approval.

All of the repositories evaluated utilized an IRB to oversee the repository practices and to ensure that patient privacy and confidentiality are protected, and most of them require researchers requesting samples to have IRB approval for their research (see Table 7.2). At EDRN, each participating institution is responsible for following the EDRN guidelines, which require that every proposal have IRB approval before being allowed to participate/collaborate in the network. EDRN thus does not have its own IRB.

Table 7.2
Institutional Review Board Profile

Repository	IRB Dedicated/ Contracted to Repository?	IRB Approval for Use of Samples	Ethics Advisory Board/Committee
CHTN	Each institution has its own IRB	Yes	Coordinating committee
TARP	NCI IRB	No	None
EDRN	Each participating institution has its own IRB	Yes	Steering committee
Philadelphia Familial Breast Cancer Registry	Fox Chase Cancer Center IRB	Yes	Informed consent working group
NHLBI	NHLBI IRB	Yes	Executive committee
AFIP	Yes	Yes	None
Duke University Breast SPORE	Duke IRB	No	None
Mayo Clinic Prostate SPORE	Mayo IRB	Yes	None
UAB Breast and Ovarian SPOREs	UAB IRB	Yes	None
University of Pittsburgh HSTB	UPMC IRB	Yes	None
Ardais	Yes	Yes	Bioethics advisory board
GCI	Yes	Yes	Bioethics advisory board

Both Ardais and GCI utilize private IRBs for research requests that do not already have IRB approval. Ardais has contracted with Independent Review Consulting (IRC). GCI currently works with two commercial IRBs, Essex IRB and Western IRB, and is always evaluating other commercial IRBs.

BBI has its own IRB. In addition, NHLBI's DCC also uses its own IRB (the Cleveland Clinic Foundation) and must pass an annual review. Each division of CHTN has its own IRB (e.g., Eastern Division uses the University of Pennsylvania IRB).

University of Pittsburgh HSTB, the SPOREs at Duke University, the Mayo Clinic, and UAB all use their own IRBs. TARP uses the IRB at NCI, and the Philadelphia Familial Breast Cancer Registry uses the IRB at FCCC.

CHTN, EDRN, NHLBI, Ardais, and GCI all require IRB review/approval to accompany researchers' proposals or requests for samples. University of Pittsburgh HSTB and Mayo Clinic Prostate SPORE also require IRB approval. Additionally, Mayo Clnic Prostate SPORE requires non-expedited approval plus a review by the Institution Bio-Specimen Approval Board.

AFIP sends all requests through either its IRB or its tissue utilization committee. Duke University Breast SPORE does not require IRB approval from researchers citing that all its samples are unidentified before distribution. TARP also does not require IRB approval, because the tissues used to make the arrays are unlinked (i.e., not linked to any personally identifying information about the tissue source, or anonymized), and therefore use of the arrays is exempt.

Requiring repositories to have IRB approval for the collection, storage, and distribution of biospecimens and associated data, and requiring researchers requesting samples to have IRB review of research projects that will use the samples are **best practices**.

Protection of Privacy and Confidentiality

In addition to IRB review and approval, all of the repositories have other guidelines, policies, and procedures in place to protect patient confidentiality. The CFRs Informatics Center, which designed the bioinformatics system, provides guidelines for data standardization and specimen anonymization, and implements network and database security, such as password protection, encryption, and firewalls. In addition, FCCC, where Philadelphia Familial Breast Cancer Registry is housed, has a Certificate of Confidentiality.

At BBI, the repository's own IRB ensures that the study is compliant with federal regulations governing research with human participants (45 C.F.R. §46). Because BBI never has any of the identifiable information, no procedures are needed to ensure that the repository maintains patient confidentiality. In addition, NHLBI's DCC undergoes its own IRB review annually. Ardais's situation is similar to BBI's in that it does not have the identifying information at the actual repository. The consenting and de-identification procedures followed at the collection sites have been subject to third-party audit and no significant issues have been found.

CHTN in general keeps all identifying information at the various collection sites it uses. CHTN and University of Pittsburgh HSTB use the "honest broker" model. The honest broker gathers data from multiple sources and replaces identifying information with a code (Merz et al., 1997). The researcher then has access only to the coded information, not to the identifying information. The Honest Broker System at University of Pittsburgh HSTB, which is IRB approved, encompasses the Health Science Tissue Bank, Clinical Outcomes, the Cancer Registry, Centers for Pathology and Oncology Informatics, and the Center for Pathology Quality and Health Care Research. The Honest Broker System, which is under the systems management officer, provides seamless communication between these departments and allows researchers to obtain tissue samples and associated data from a single source.

CHTN uses many other strategies to ensure patient confidentiality, including IRB oversight, coding, parsing to verify data prior to unlinking, vulnerability assessment, and automated encryption or delinking. University of Pittsburgh HSTB employs both physical and cyber security measures (e.g., shredders, guards, firewalls, and passwords) to protect personal patient information. Some of these strategies may also be employed by other repositories, but they are all useful as specific examples of possible ways to approach these issues.

TARP, which receives many of its samples from CHTN, generally does not keep identifying information with the specimens in the laboratory for the publicly available tissue microarrays. One collaborative study that is currently ongoing does use identifiable information, but it is accessible by only two people. This limited-access strategy generally is used in all of the repositories at which identifiable information is kept on site. At Duke University Breast SPORE, only two people have access to information linking patients to specimens. The database containing this information is otherwise protected by passwords in a locked room.

The UAB Breast and Ovarian SPOREs keep all personally identifying information in a separate log that is not accessible on line. For identified specimens, GCI uses a third party that has signed a legal contract to keep the information confidential. Limiting access to the codes that link patients' identifying information to their tissue specimens through physical and/or cyber procedures to minimize the chance of identifying information being released is a **best practice**. This is practiced at CHTN, EDRN, NHLBI, the UAB Breast and Ovarian SPOREs, University of Pittsburgh HSTB, Ardais, and GCI.

In addition to IRB oversight, several repositories also rely on separate review boards or committees to oversee their privacy and confidentiality procedures: CHTN, EDRN, Philadelphia Familial Breast Cancer Registry, AFIP, Ardais, and GCI. CHTN has a coordinating committee and the Breast and Ovarian CFR has a steering committee to oversee these procedures. At EDRN it is a data sharing and informatics subcommittee that meets to develop security systems and safeguards for protecting patient privacy. GCI has a bioethics advisory board, which follows the standards and guidelines set out by the NBAC. Ardais also has a bioethics advisory board. AFIP follows Department of Defense guidelines that incorporate HIPAA and regulate the use of human participants in research. Having a bioethics advisory board or other governance and oversight board/committee to oversee privacy and confidentiality procedures is a **best practice** that provides another layer of review.

Impact of Federal and State Privacy Laws

The new HIPAA regulations regarding privacy of individually identifiable health information could have significant impact on tissue repositories. Most of the repositories evaluated have had to modify their procedures to some extent as a result of HIPAA. One exception is AFIP, where the procedures already in place reportedly exceeded HIPAA requirements, so no further changes were necessary. Research at TARP is exempt under HIPAA because the data are de-identified, and BBI reported that it has not made any changes yet but is expecting some to take place soon—for instance, with regard to the few specimens in the repository that may have patient identifiers on them (note that these were not necessarily specimens from NHLBI-sponsored studies).

Both Ardais and GCI have addressed the new HIPAA requirements for an authorization form to be given to the institutions serving as collection sites. Both have implemented new procedures for this requirement. Although Ardais mentioned that it is not a covered entity under HIPAA, it has utilized the HIPAA concept of a "data use agreement" and the "limited data set" to address transmissibility of certain types of protected health information. GCI noted that the two types of information it collects that are covered by the new HIPAA regulations (town name and date of procedure) are used by the repository for verification purposes only and are not shared with repository users. Likewise, the UAB Breast and Ovarian SPOREs have purged their system of all dates, including dates of medical treatment and birth dates. At Duke University Breast SPORE the practice of reviewing the operating room schedules to identify potential tissue sources was stopped. Now, patients are initially approached by their own physician about donating tissue, and repository personnel then follow up with the patient to get his or her consent. EDRN faced a somewhat unique challenge. A significant portion of the EDRN specimens existed at universities prior to EDRN being established but are now available through the network. Most of the changes that were required in response to HIPAA applied to these earlier collections.

CHTN has begun providing a limited data set to researchers and using data-use agreements that researchers must sign in order to obtain samples. Philadelphia Familial Breast Cancer Registry amended its consent form following HIPAA implementation. However, it was noted that these new procedures have not changed the way the research is done.

AFIP, BBI, Duke, TARP, and University of Pittsburgh HSTB all reported that state laws have had no impact on their repositories. Ardais and EDRN have each responded differently to the challenge of having to comply with state laws for collection sites. Ardais has avoided establishing collection relationships with institutions in the two to three states it has determined have ambiguous laws. EDRN requires every participating collection site to comply with state laws before it joins the network.

Philadelphia Familial Breast Cancer Registry reported that New York state law does not allow genetic testing results from a laboratory outside New York State to be given to individuals residing in New York State. The UAB Breast and Ovarian SPOREs also mentioned that Florida state law requires specific consent from each patient for genetic testing.

A Minnesota state law requiring consent to review a patient's health records significantly affected Mayo Clinic Prostate SPORE. Now all patients must specifically consent to having their medical records used for research.

CHTN overall is not affected by state laws, but each individual collection site must comply with its own state laws. GCI has examined the state laws and believes that in most cases federal law supercedes them.

Consent Issues

Informed consent is a key mechanism for protecting the interests, welfare, and rights of research participants. Informed consent is a process, not just a form, that educates and provides information to potential research participants about details of the research, including potential benefits and risks, procedures, duration, and more, in language they can understand. The informed consent process enables individuals to decide voluntarily whether or not to participate in research.

AFIP and CHTN primarily collect specimens with a general surgical consent. Specimens submitted to AFIP were originally obtained by pathology departments at the hospitals where the patients underwent medical treatment. Therefore, the submitting institution, and not AFIP, determines the actual informed consent process. Most CHTN divisions operate under a waiver of consent, and the specimens are collected with a general surgical consent that indicates that the specimens may be used for research. The operating procedures for each CHTN division have been reviewed by each institution's IRB to ensure that they meet all of the requirements of current regulations for the protection of research participants. The specific operating procedures, however, vary depending upon the requirements of the IRB at each division and/or collection site, and some CHTN divisions obtain specific consent from individuals for the use of their tissue. For example, the Pediatric Division of CHTN obtains informed consent for research use of tissue that is collected as part of pediatric clinical trials. Western Division, at Vanderbilt University, provides only unlinked (anonymized) specimens.

At all of the repositories evaluated where specific informed consent is obtained for the collection of biospecimens, it is obtained separately from the surgical consent. At Ardais, consent is obtained specifically for the collection of tissue specimens for research purposes. This consent is for general research, in the sense that the tissue is being collected without a specific research project in mind. The consent document delineates several protocols supporting research and discovery into diagnostics and therapeutics, and asks for permission to go into the patient's health records pertaining to the diagnosis for which the surgery was being performed. Since the passage of the Minnesota state law mentioned above, the consent document for Mayo Clinic Prostate SPORE also asks for permission to review a patient's health records. Mayo Clinic Prostate SPORE also uses a consent template that combines a specific project with a general research area. Obtaining tissue specimens from individuals who are fully informed about and have consented to the collection of their tissue by the repository and its use for research purposes is a **best practice**.[3]

---

[3] It may not always be possible to obtain full informed consent for the research use of tissue. In its report *Research Involving Human Biological Materials: Ethical Issues and Policy Guidance*, NBAC found that when important research with human biological materials poses little or no risk to participants whose consent would be difficult or impossible to obtain, it is appropriate for the IRB to waive the consent requirement (NBAC, 1999). In addition, current federal regulations governing research with human participants (45 C.F.R. §46; the Common Rule) state that research with human participants is presumed to require consent,

Ideally, the consent process should occur separately from the surgical consent. However, this is not always possible, so at a minimum, the informed consent for the collection and research use of specimens should be a separate section of the surgical consent form that requires a separate signature.

A few repositories use consent processes that offer individuals who would like to donate tissue some options for limiting the use of their tissue and/or medical information. GCI's consent is slightly different in that individuals who contribute blood are given the option of limiting the use of their specimens solely to research pertaining to the disease for which they were being treated at the time the specimen was collected. This option is not offered for tissue specimens at GCI. At University of Pittsburgh HSTB, the specimens in the repository come with one of three different types of consent: (1) use of the tissue for a specific research project, (2) global consent (not tissue or research specific), or (3) non-consented anonymized collection. At UAB, individuals give specific consent for donation of tissue to the Breast or the Ovarian SPORE but can opt out of donating blood and the use of their tissue for genetic research. Likewise, at Duke University Breast SPORE, individuals considering donating to the repository are given the option of consenting to the use of blood products or tissue samples, or both. Mayo Clinic Prostate SPORE also uses a tiered consent process that allows individuals to choose what their tissue can be used for. Sometimes, CHTN also uses a tiered consent process. Performing a tiered consent process that allows individuals to choose the type of specimen(s), if any, they want to donate (e.g., tissue, blood, or urine), the type of research the specimen can be used for (e.g., a specific research project, general research, or genetic research), and/or whether their medical records and outcomes data can be accessed is a **best practice**.

---

but that this requirement can be altered or waived by the IRB if all four of the following criteria, set forth at 45 C.F.R. §46.116(d), are met: (1) The research involves no more than minimal risk to participants, (2) the waiver or alteration of consent will not adversely affect the rights and welfare of participants, (3) the research could not practicably be carried out without the waiver or alteration, and (4) whenever appropriate, participants will be provided with additional pertinent information after participation.

CHTN, Philadelphia Familial Breast Cancer Registry, NHLBI, Duke University Breast SPORE, Mayo Clinic Prostate SPORE, the UAB Breast and Ovarian SPOREs, University of Pittsburgh HSTB, Ardais, and GCI all use consent interviews. The consent process varies among CHTN divisions and even among collection sites, since all consent processes must be approved by each institution's IRB. Whether EDRN uses a consent interview is determined by the collection site and depends on the study being conducted. Who is responsible for consent interviews at each repository and when the consent process is undertaken are detailed in Table 7.3.

Best Practices

1. Limit access to the codes that link patients' identifying information to their tissue specimens through physical and/or cyber procedures to minimize the chance of identifying information being released. This is practiced at all of the repositories.
2. Require repositories to have IRB approval for the collection, storage, and distribution of biospecimens and associated data, and require researchers requesting samples to have IRB review of research projects that will use the samples. All of the repositories have IRB oversight of repository practices. All of the repositories except Duke and TARP, which distribute only samples with de-identified data, require researchers requesting samples to have IRB review of their research.
3. Use a bioethics advisory board or other governance and oversight advisory board to provide another layer of review for privacy and confidentiality procedures. All of the repositories use IRBs to oversee privacy and confidentiality. In addition, CHTN, EDRN, Philadelphia Familial Breast Cancer Registry, AFIP, Ardais, and GCI have some type of advisory board that oversees privacy and confidentiality issues.
4. Obtain tissue specimens from individuals who are fully informed about and have consented to both the collection of their tissue by the repository and its use for research purposes. Ideally, the con-

Table 7.3
Individuals Conducting Consent Interviews

Repository	Individual Conducting Consent Interview	When Consent Is Obtained
CHTN	CHTN staff, surgeon, resident, nurse, or admitting staff	Before and after surgery
EDRN	Study and site dependent (e.g., principal investigator, nurse, social workers)	Study and site dependent
Philadelphia Familial Breast Cancer Registry	Health educator or genetic counselor	At time of CFR enrollment
NHLBI	LAM study coordinator, principal investigator, or histotechnologist	At time of LAM registry enrollment
Duke University Breast SPORE	Trained phlebotomist	Before surgery
Mayo Clinic Prostate SPORE	RN	24 hours after surgery for prostate tissue; before surgery for other tissue
UAB Breast and Ovarian SPOREs	Experienced research nurse, or biorepository staff	Before surgery
University of Pittsburgh HSTB	Principal investigator or clinical staff	Before surgery (varies by project)
Ardais	Experienced research nurse	Before surgery (varies by institution)
GCI	Designated FTE at each collection site	Before surgery

sent process should occur separately from the surgical consent. However, this is not always possible, so at a minimum, the informed consent for the collection and research use of specimens should be a separate section of the surgical consent form that requires a separate signature. EDRN, NHLBI, Philadelphia Familial Breast Cancer Registry, Duke University Breast SPORE, Mayo Clinic Prostate SPORE, the UAB Breast and Ovarian SPOREs, University of Pittsburgh HSTB, Ardais, and GCI primarily collect biospecimens from individuals who have specifically consented to the collection and research use of their tissue.

5. Perform a tiered consent process that allows individuals to choose the type of specimen(s), if any, they want to donate (e.g., tissue, blood, or urine), the type of research the specimen can be used for (e.g., a specific research project, general research, or genetic research), and/or whether their medical records and outcomes data can be accessed. Duke University Breast SPORE, Mayo Clinic Prostate SPORE, the UAB Breast and Ovarian SPOREs, and GCI all use a tiered informed consent process. CHTN also occasionally uses a tiered consent process.

CHAPTER EIGHT

Intellectual Property and Legal Issues

The repositories' practices and procedures are generally based on the presence of developed standards and policies associated with research involving human participants, and it seems that few problems have been encountered regarding intellectual property or liability. In this chapter, we describe some of the specific mechanisms the institutions have in place to ensure that these policies and procedures are clear and consistent.

Policies Regarding Intellectual Property Rights

The majority of repositories do not retain any intellectual property rights to the samples they distribute, unless they are performing the research in collaboration with other researchers, in which case the intellectual property rights are shared. Similarly, institutions that contribute specimens to the repository do not retain any intellectual property rights to tissue they submit. For repositories located at academic institutions, much of the tissue collected is used by researchers from that institution, in which case the institution does control intellectual property rights. This, however, is based on the *researcher's* affiliation with the institution, not the *tissue's* affiliation.

The Breast and Ovarian CFRs, of which the Philadelphia Familial Breast Cancer Registry is a member, is the only repository evaluated that specifically maintains intellectual property rights to the data it collects. As stated in the CFRs' *Access Policies and Procedures*

Manual: "CFRs sites retain custody of, and have primary rights to, data collected under their current NIH awards, subject to Government rights of access and consistent with current DHHS, Public Health Service (PHS), and NIH policies" (Cancer Family Registries, 2002).

CHTN takes no ownership position on intellectual property created using its specimens. TARP has determined that its tissue microarrays are not patentable because they are functionally a single- or limited-use reagent with no inherent intellectual property value. AFIP also has no specific policies in place that address intellectual property. It receives tissue under medical consultative conditions and believes that the relinquishment or transfer of tissue from patient to surgeon/pathologist at the surgical level and from pathologist to AFIP at the secondary consultative level, with no conditions on continued possession, are both irrevocable donations or gifts that transfer ownership ultimately to AFIP.

Duke also has no specific intellectual property policies for the distribution of tissue. However, collaborative research with Duke researchers becomes Duke University's intellectual property. Similarly at GCI the fee-for-service researchers retain the intellectual property rights; however, intellectual property rights with GCI collaborators are negotiated on a case-by-case basis. At University of Pittsburgh HSTB, the institution where the research takes place retains the intellectual property rights, so the university retains them for research conducted by its researchers, and private-sector companies retain them for research conducted by their researchers. Similarly, Ardais does not retain intellectual property rights for discoveries made using tissue it distributes. Ardais conducted significant legal research to develop a licensing mechanism to transfer samples and data from the repository to researchers, ensuring clear ownership of intellectual property developed from sample use.

The tissue microarrays made by TARP are treated as reagents with no inherent intellectual property value. However, tissue microarrays made using the NCI-60 cell lines or xenografts are protected intellectual property and require the use of a materials transfer agreement (MTA). Mayo requires MTAs for its tissue, and all sharing is coordinated through the Mayo Medical Ventures group, a venture capital investing program that tries to find markets for medical research conducted at the Mayo Clinic.

As a network of university researchers, EDRN follows the guidelines laid out in the Bayh-Dole law mandating that the intellectual property rights for work done by university researchers using government funding and support belong to the researchers. In addition, EDRN requires that any pre-existing agreements that a participant has regarding intellectual property or exclusive licenses must not prevent collaboration within EDRN.

To promote clarity, to prevent potential legal confusion, and to avoid conflicts with tissue sources, researchers using tissue, and institutions contributing biospecimens, it is a **best practice** to use a specific published policy on intellectual property regarding research use of samples from a repository.

Rights of Tissue Source and Contributing Institutions to Tissue

Tissue sources usually have a right to withdraw their consent and have their tissue removed from the repository if the specimens are identifiable. This is a requirement in the Common Rule (45 C.R.F. §46) for all federally funded research. Individuals donating tissue to CHTN, Philadelphia Familial Breast Cancer Registry, NHLBI, AFIP, Duke University Breast SPORE, Mayo Clinic Prostate SPORE, the UAB Breast and Ovarian SPOREs, University of Pittsburgh HSTB, Ardais, and GCI have the right to withdraw consent for the use of their tissue. EDRN's policies are institution specific. When tissue and data are stripped of identifiers and records are destroyed (unlinked samples)—as is the case (1) at GCI once the 30-day window during which a specimen is linked to the tissue source's identity has expired, and (2) at TARP, which does not receive identifying information with the tissue samples it gets from CHTN—then it is not possible for tissue sources to withdraw their tissue from the repository.

Removing a tissue source's specimen from the repository also means ensuring that computer records are not maintained for that person. Ardais's solution to this issue is to perform monthly backups of their computer systems and bioinformatics system. The backup from the previous month is then destroyed, so that when information about a tissue source is removed from the system, the information is not maintained on any backup tapes. Tissue and data that have already been distributed become unlinked (anonymized). In the LAM study at NHLBI, tissue sources also have the right to have their tissue sent to a specific investigator. Other than this, however, at no repositories do tissue sources have the right to request that their tissue be returned to them or that specific studies be performed on their tissue. A **best practice** in the area of rights to tissue by the tissue source is to allow the withdrawal of consent and have the tissue, data, and computer records removed from the repository if the tissue retains identifiers to link it to the tissue source and has not already been distributed to researchers.

Institutions similarly give up their rights to the tissue they have contributed to a repository in most cases. However, several repositories, including Ardais and GCI, give the contributing institutions priority for tissue requests. Similarly, at Mayo Clinic Prostate SPORE, internal researchers have first right to the tissue they provide.[1]

Compensation

Generally, tissue sources are not compensated financially, unless the tissue collection is part of a clinical trial that compensates the participants. For specimens collected by CHTN, TARP, Philadelphia Familial Breast Cancer Registry, the NHLBI LAM study, AFIP, Duke University Breast SPORE, Mayo Clinic Prostate SPORE, the UAB Breast and Ovarian SPOREs, University of Pittsburgh HSTB, and Ardais, tissue sources are not compensated in any way. At EDRN, the

---

[1] See Chapter Five for a complete discussion of prioritization policies at each repository.

policies are institution specific. At GCI, tissue sources are generally not compensated except in a very few cases where they have been reimbursed for time and travel.

Agreements Used in Tissue Distribution

In many cases the researchers must sign a formal agreement to obtain tissue. At CHTN, researchers sign the Agreement for Use of Tissue, in which they agree that the samples will be used only for the purposes cited in the application, no attempt to obtain identifying information will be made, no specimens will be sold or shared with a third party without the prior written permission of CHTN, they recognize that all specimens should be treated as potentially infectious, they will ensure proper training of all those who will be handling the specimens, there is no implied warranty on the tissue specimens, they are required to acknowledge the use of CHTN specimens in any publications, and they vest liability for any injury involving the use of the specimens to the extent permitted by law with the recipient. CHTN's Agreement for Use of Tissue was approved by the Office of the General Counsel of DHHS. TARP uses the same agreement. When obtaining samples from Ardais, researchers and entities sign contracts that include license applications, restrictions on use, and data use agreements (i.e., to support HIPAA requirements). EDRN, Mayo Clinic Prostate SPORE, and GCI require recipients to sign material transfer agreements. The use of a tissue use agreement is a **best practice**. The tissue use agreements should contain language in which researchers agree that the specimens will be used only for the purposes cited in the application, no attempt to obtain identifying information will be made, no specimens will be sold or shared with a third party without the prior written permission of the repository, all specimens will be treated as potentially infectious, all personnel who will be handling the specimens will be properly trained, there is no implied warranty on the specimens, any publications resulting from the use of repository specimens will acknowledge the repository, and the researcher/institution using the tissue assumes responsibility for all risks associated with the receipt, handling, storage, and use of the tissue.

The NHLBI LAM study does not require researchers to sign an agreement to obtain most samples (i.e., for samples that are unlinked from any identifying information about the tissue source). However, if there are clinical data associated with the sample, an agreement between the researcher and the registry must be signed. NHLBI LAM is planning to use agreements in future studies.

Liability Issues

In most cases, liability for the use of tissue lies with the researcher, based on the contract signed to receive the tissue, as described above. None of the repositories has experienced liability issues regarding safety issues associated with the use of the specimens, loss of privacy, or breach of confidentiality of tissue sources, claims by tissue sources of physical/psychosocial harms, or claims by tissue sources to property rights for discoveries made using their tissue. Even so, it is a **best practice** to specify the responsibility for assuming risks in connection with the use of biospecimens in tissue use agreements, to fully inform tissue sources about risks to their rights and welfare, and to clarify ownership issues during the informed consent process.

Ensuring Responsible Use of Resources

In addition to the agreements discussed above, all of the repositories used various means to ensure that tissue is distributed to legitimate researchers and organizations. Inspection of IRB documentation, review of the study design for which the samples will be used, verification that the researcher requesting samples is associated with a legitimate research institution, and, in some cases, personal knowledge of researchers in a specific field allow the repositories to be sure that the recipients are legitimate. It is a **best practice** to carefully review researcher credentials and submissions, including IRB documentation, to ensure that legitimate researchers are using tissue for legitimate purposes.

Best Practices

1. Use an explicit intellectual property policy to prevent potential legal confusion and contention. Philadelphia Familial Breast Cancer Registry follows the Cancer Family Registries' policy on intellectual property that is stated explicitly.
2. Allow tissue sources to withdraw samples if they are not unlinked or have not already been distributed to researchers. This is the policy at CHTN, Philadelphia Familial Breast Cancer Registry, NHLBI (for the LAM study), AFIP, Duke University Breast SPORE, Mayo Clinic Prostate SPORE, the UAB Breast and Ovarian SPOREs, University of Pittsburgh HSTB, Ardais, and GCI (within the 30-day window).
3. Use a tissue use agreement that contains language in which researchers agree that the specimens will be used only for the purposes cited in the application, no attempt to obtain identifying information will be made, no specimens will be sold or shared with a third party without the prior written permission of the repository, all specimens will be treated as potentially infectious, all personnel who will be handling the specimens will be properly trained, there is no implied warranty on the specimens, any publications resulting from the use of repository specimens will acknowledge the repository, and the researcher/institution using the tissue assumes responsibility for all risks associated with the receipt, handling, storage, and use of the tissue. The Tissue Use Agreement used by CHTN is a good example of this.
4. Explicitly specify the responsibility for assuming risks in connection with the use of biospecimens in tissue use agreements, fully inform tissue sources about risks to their rights and welfare, and clarify ownership issues during the informed consent process. CHTN, TARP, University of Pittsburgh HSTB, and Ardais spec-

ify the responsibility for assuming risks in connection with the use of biospecimens in their tissue use agreements.

5. Perform a careful review of researcher requests, as is conducted by all of the repositories evaluated, to determine researcher credentials and to ensure responsible use of samples. This review should include the inspection of IRB documentation, review of the study design for which the samples will be used, and verification that the researcher requesting samples is associated with a legitimate research institution.

CHAPTER NINE

Public Relations, Marketing, and Education

Public relations, marketing, and education are critical to the success of large tissue repositories and repositories for rare conditions. The repositories evaluated use a combination of approaches to increase the visibility of their resource and mission.

Marketing

The repositories use a variety of means to market themselves to researchers, including advertisements in major journals (e.g., *Science* and *Nature*), exhibits at appropriate professional conferences, direct mailings, word of mouth, and Web sites for the repositories and associated clinical trials and research projects. Some of the smaller repositories do not market themselves at all. CHTN uses exhibits at scientific meetings and mailings to researchers attending the meetings, fliers, the NIH Research Festival, journal advertisements, its Web site, and a newsletter to researchers called "Tissue Topics" to market its resource. EDRN also sponsors exhibits at many major scientific conferences that are related to its mission. In addition, EDRN has advertised in *JAMA* and *Science*, mostly during its first year. Ardais and GCI also use several of these approaches, including exhibits at meetings, advertising in journals, and word of mouth. In addition, Ardais sponsors a seminar series on clinical genomics. The NHLBI LAM study has effectively used word of mouth, and the LAM Foundation usually has an exhibit at various medical conferences. In addition to advertising the resource at national meetings, AFIP produces a newsletter six times a year that has a broad distribution to 17,000 pathologists, 5,000 of whom are outside the United States. AFIP also produces both an annual report and an annual research progress report. AFIP is currently developing a new business and marketing plan. Duke and Mayo do not directly market their resources, instead relying on word of mouth. While University of Pittsburgh HSTB has been a part of marketing efforts by CPCTR (at an exhibit at the American Association for Cancer Research [AACR] meeting), most of its exposure is by word of mouth. Using a combination of the methods discussed above—such as exhibits at scientific meetings, word of mouth, Web sites, newsletters, and advertising in scientific journals—to market the repository's resources represents a **best practice**.

Few repositories have any marketing strategies for recruiting patients. University of Pittsburgh HSTB has benefited from word of mouth at prostate cancer support groups. FCCC, where Philadelphia Familial Breast Cancer Registry is located, has brochures about its Biosample Repository in its patient waiting room. GCI has information for individuals interested in contributing tissue to the repository on its Web site.

Outreach, Patient Education, and Post-Research Communications

Few of the repositories have active education for and communication with individuals who have donated tissue. EDRN invites patient advocates to all of its workshops, but any communication with tissue sources is institution specific. This is also true for the NHLBI LAM study. The LAM Foundation sponsors scientific and patient workshops, which report back generalized findings that result from the studies, but communication with tissue sources is specific to the individual clinical centers. Similarly, University of Pittsburgh HSTB does not target specific patients, instead disseminating research news and patient education information on its general Web site (www.upmccancercenters.com), including cancer information and current clinical trials. University of Pittsburgh HSTB has also disseminated research results on the Reuters news wire. The Mayo Clinic has a Web site (http://www.mayoclinic.com) that contains information for cancer patients. GCI sponsors continuing medical education workshops for all physicians in GCI's Physician Network. Philadelphia Familial Breast Cancer Registry sends a quarterly newsletter to registry participants that summarizes research with registry resources and announces new research projects. Although not widely done today, a **best practice** for repositories is to provide information about generalized findings that result from research with repository resources to tissue sources and physicians through the Internet, newsletters, and sessions at scientific meetings, or through other outreach venues.

In some cases, if repository personnel make a diagnosis of a specimen that differs from the one in the pathology report, the repository notifies the pathologist on record and/or the attending physician to ensure that patient care is optimal. Both Philadelphia Familial Breast Cancer Registry and the Mayo Clinic also state in their informed consent that physicians might contact tissue sources if a genetic study shows something that might be clinically relevant.

Best Practices

1. Use a combination of methods—such as exhibits at scientific meetings, word of mouth, Web sites, newsletters, and advertising in scientific journals—to market the repository's resources. CHTN, EDRN, NHLBI, AFIP, University of Pittsburgh HSTB, Ardais, and GCI use all of these methods.
2. Provide information about generalized findings that result from research with repository resources to tissue sources and physicians through the Internet, newsletters, sessions at scientific meetings, or through other outreach venues. NHLBI LAM Registry, Mayo Clinic, University of Pittsburgh HSTB, Philadelphia Familial Breast Cancer Registry, and GCI provide generalized information to tissue sources and/or physicians.

CHAPTER TEN

Findings and Summary of Best Practices

Findings

Each of the repositories evaluated for this study was established to fulfill specific needs, and its procedures and operations were designed to enable it to do so. Thus, each repository's design is integrally linked to the needs it was established to fulfill. Table 10.1 summarizes the findings presented in Chapters Three through Nine for each of the repositories evaluated for this study. The design and operation of each repository and other relevant findings are detailed in the first half of this chapter.

Cooperative Human Tissue Network

CHTN is an NCI-funded repository that prospectively collects and distributes over 60,000 tissue samples per year to academic, government, and industry researchers. Approximately 80 percent of the tissue collected by CHTN is distributed to academic and government researchers. The bioinformatics system used by CHTN was designed as a repository management tool to track specimen collection, characterization (histopathology), and distribution. The majority of tissue collected by CHTN is from patients who are undergoing surgical or other diagnostic procedures and have given general surgical consent for the use of their tissue for research and education purposes. Most CHTN divisions operate under a waiver of consent; however, the specific procedures vary depending on the requirements of the IRB at each division and/or collection site. CHTN takes no position on

Table 10.1
Summary of Findings

Repository	Tissue Repository Design	Bioinformatics	Consumers/ Users	Opera- tions	Privacy, Ethical, and Consent Issues	Intellectual Property and Legal Issues	Public Relations, Marketing, and Education
CHTN	Prospective collection/ distribution; limited banking of pediatric and/or rare specimens	Repository and pathological/ clinical data management	80% academic; 20% commer- cial (Eastern Division: 68% academic + NIH + hospitals; 32% industry)	Publicly funded	Consent waived; IRB approval required; use honest brokers	No IP position; agreement for use of tissue	Active marketing; no communica- tion or education
TARP	Re-processor and reposi- tory	Repository and pathological/ clinical data management; research tool for collaborative studies	60% academic; 20% NIH; 20% industry	Publicly funded	Consent waived; exempt from IRB approval	No IP position; agreement for use of tissue	Active marketing; no communica- tion or education

Table 10.1 (continued)

Repository	Tissue Repository Design	Bioinformatics	Consumers/ Users	Opera- tions	Privacy, Ethical, and Consent Issues	Intellectual Property and Legal Issues	Public Relations, Marketing, and Education
EDRN	Prospective collection	Repository and pathological/ clinical data management; combine/ standardize information from collection sites	EDRN mem- bers, who are mostly aca- demic; some private col- laborations	Publicly funded	Study dependent	Study investi- gators own IP; material transfer agreement	Active marketing; patient advocate participation
Philadelphia Familial Breast Cancer Registry	Banking	Repository and pathological/ clinical data management; research tool	~99% aca- demic	Publicly funded (NCI grant)	Informed consent; IRB review required	CFRs sites retain custody of, and have primary rights to, data; assurance form	Limited marketing (Web site, brochure); newsletter to registry participants

Table 10.1 (continued)

Repository	Tissue Repository Design	Bioinformatics	Consumers/ Users	Opera- tions	Privacy, Ethical, and Consent Issues	Intellectual Property and Legal Issues	Public Relations, Marketing, and Education
NHLBI	Study-driven banking	BBI—repository management	100% govern- ment and its collaborators	Publicly funded	Determined by study protocol	No legal/ contractual agreement for use of LAM Registry samples	No active marketing; no communica- tion or education
AFIP	Diagnostic center	Repository management; limited clinical data manage- ment	Primarily pathologists	Research is sec- ondary to diag- nostics	General surgical consent; IRB or tissue utilization committee	No IP position; agreement for use of patho-logical material	Limited marketing (Web site, meetings); newsletter to pathology community
Duke University Breast SPORE	Prospective and banking	Repository and pathological/ clinical data management	80% academic; 20% govern- ment	Primarily publicly funded	Informed consent; IRB approval not required for use of unlinked samples	IP belongs to Duke for collaborative research; no legal/ contractual agreement	No active marketing; no communica- tion or education

Table 10.1 (continued)

Repository	Tissue Repository Design	Bioinformatics	Consumers/ Users	Opera- tions	Privacy, Ethical, and Consent Issues	Intellectual Property and Legal Issues	Public Relations, Marketing, and Education
Mayo Clinic Prostate SPORE	Prospective and banking	Repository and pathological/ clinical data management; research tool	90–95% Mayo	Primarily publicly funded	Informed con- sent; full IRB approval required	IP position based on material transfer agreement	No active marketing; no communicatio n or education
UAB Breast and Ovarian SPOREs	Banking	Repository and pathological/ clinical data management	90% academic; 10% industry	Publicly funded (NCI grant)	Informed consent; IRB review required	No IP position; tissue use agreement	Only inter- nally at UAB through conferences; no communi- cation or education

Table 10.1 (continued)

Repository	Tissue Repository Design	Bioinformatics	Consumers/ Users	Opera- tions	Privacy, Ethical, and Consent Issues	Intellectual Property and Legal Issues	Public Relations, Marketing, and Education
University of Pittsburgh HTSB	Prospective and banking	Repository and pathological/ clinical data management; integrate multiple sites and extract data; research tool	90% UPMC researchers	Primarily publicly funded	Informed consent; IRB approval required; uses honest brokers	IP belongs to UPMC for research done by its faculty or to commercial clients who pay for service	Limited marketing (Web site, meetings); host of annual Frontiers in Oncology and Pathology Informatics meeting
Ardais	Banking	Repository and pathological/ clinical data management	Academic medical centers; biotech and pharmaceutical companies	Primarily private; some public grant money	Informed consent; IRB approval required	No IP position; research use application and access agreement	Active marketing; sponsors seminar series on clinical genomics

Table 10.1 (continued)

Repository	Tissue Repository Design	Bioinformatics	Consumers/ Users	Operations	Privacy, Ethical, and Consent Issues	Intellectual Property and Legal Issues	Public Relations, Marketing, and Education
GCI	Internal/ collaborative research; fee-for-service banking and distribution to fund research	Repository and pathological/ clinical data management; research tool	Mostly industry (~65%) on fee-for-service side; government and academic collaborators	Research is primary mission	Informed consent; third party used for maintaining links to tissue source ID	IP belongs to fee-for-service customers or is shared among internal/ collaborator researchers; material transfer agreement	Active marketing; continuing medical education workshops for physicians in its physician network

intellectual property. Researchers sign the Agreement for Use of Tissue to use the CHTN resources and accept liability for the use of the resources in this agreement. CHTN actively markets its resource but has no communication with or educational activities for patients from whom biospecimens are collected. Other findings of interest at CHTN are:

- CHTN efficiently and effectively prospectively collects and distributes approximately 60,000 samples per year to hundreds of researchers across the United States and Canada. This is by far the greatest number of samples distributed by the twelve repositories evaluated. In addition, CHTN uses standard protocols for the collection, processing, annotation, storage, and distribution of specimens, which are quasi-customized to meet a host of researcher needs. The decentralized collection, storage, and distribution model, with the regional divisions responsible for their own regions but also networked to help satisfy the unmet needs of researchers in other regions, increases access to a wide variety of specimen types.
- Repositories that bank tissues are subject to certain constraints because they store tissue using current technology, which can make it difficult to plan for future technologies. Because CHTN is not a bank, it is not limited by these constraints.
- The CHTN Coordinating Committee, made up of the principal investigator of each regional division, an additional member from each division, and a representative from NCI, formulates policies for the operation of CHTN. This committee meets periodically to assess the operation of CHTN and to change or modify operating policies.
- CHTN takes feedback from its users seriously. A feedback questionnaire is enclosed with each shipment, allowing the researcher to provide rapid feedback about the quality of that particular shipment. This information helps highlight any problems and allows CHTN to address them immediately. A more detailed questionnaire is sent annually to researchers who receive tissue from CHTN. The information collected in this annual evalua-

tion is used to identify positive features that should be maintained and problems that should be corrected.

- CHTN actively participates in national discussions of legal and ethical issues related to the collection and use of human biospecimens for research purposes.

Tissue Array Research Program

The TARP laboratory, located at NCI, receives paraffin-embedded tissues from CHTN and uses them to produce tissue microarrays that are distributed to researchers through the CHTN Eastern Division. The TARP laboratory is also involved in many collaborative research efforts for which collaborators provide specialized tissues for incorporation into tissue microarrays. Approximately 60 percent of the tissue microarrays distributed by TARP are distributed to academic researchers, approximately 20 percent go to NIH researchers, and approximately 20 percent go to private industry researchers. TARP's bioinformatics system is primarily used for repository management purposes, but it is designed to be a research tool and is used as such for some of the collaborative studies. TARP follows the guidelines of CHTN when it comes to privacy, ethical and consent issues, with one exception: It does not require IRB approval for the use of its arrays, because the arrays are made from unlinked tissue (i.e., tissue not linked to any personally identifying information about the tissue source, anonymized) and are therefore exempt. TARP has concluded that its tissue microarrays are not patentable because the microarrays are functionally a single- or limited-use reagent with no inherent intellectual property value. TARP actively markets its resource, but has no communication with or education activities for tissue sources after they have contributed tissue. Other relevant findings at TARP are:

- TARP produces and distributes multitumor tissue microarrays for cancer researchers and is at the center of developing related technology for use in high-throughput screening of DNA, RNA, and protein targets in multiple tumor tissues using immunohistochemical, in situ hybridization, and fluorescence in situ hybridization (FISH) analysis.

- TARP arrays contain approximately 500 tissue samples, whereas arrays available from commercial businesses usually contain only 80 to 100 tissue samples. TARP arrays also contain smaller cores and a much higher density of tissue samples than commercially available arrays do, and they cost significantly less. (TARP charges academic researchers $40 per slide and commercial researchers $120 per slide; commercially available arrays can cost $150 to $200 per slide.)

Early Detection Research Network

EDRN is a collection of over 40 primarily academic research centers and a dozen private industry partners that facilitates collaborative research to link the discovery of biomarkers directly to the next steps of developing early detection tests. Collection, processing, and annotation of specimens and data reporting are all standardized. The combined repository of all the participants is available through the network. EDRN is funded through NCI and conducts "just in time" specimen collection based on the research needs. Privacy, ethical, and consent issues must be addressed and IRB approved prior to a research study being funded. The study investigators own any resulting intellectual property rights. EDRN actively markets at conferences and in journals. Other findings of interest are that:

- EDRN represents a good example of collaborative research, the whole being greater than the sum of its parts. EDRN's business model of a virtual repository enhances sample availability and information sharing among researchers. The specimens it counts in its collection are stored at geographically dispersed collection sites, but the data and information regarding these specimens are maintained centrally.
- The participants of EDRN agree to a standardized method of collection and reporting. Therefore, each network participant has access to the database of all the other participants for the purposes of furthering cancer research.

Philadelphia Familial Breast Cancer Registry

Philadelphia Familial Breast Cancer Registry is part of the Breast and Ovarian CFRs, an NCI-funded network of international registries that collects extensive epidemiological medical data and biospecimens from breast and ovarian cancer patients and their families. The CFRs are collecting and banking blood and tumor specimens for use in epidemiological and genetic research. Virtually all of the specimens collected by the CFRs are used by academic researchers. Biospecimens are collected by the CFRs with specific informed consent for participation in the registries, and researchers are required to have IRB approval for research that uses CFR resources. Unlike several of the other repositories, the CFR sites retain custody of and have primary rights to data generated through the use of CFR resources. This is primarily through collaborative agreements between CFR researchers and other academic researchers. The CFRs market their resources primarily through word of mouth, their Web site, and a brochure developed by NCI. The CFRs communicate with individuals who participate in the registries through a newsletter, distributed every four months, that summarizes research by the registries and announces new research projects. The CFRs also inform participants of any clinically relevant test results that may be performed with their tissues. Other interesting aspects of Philadelphia Familial Breast Cancer Registry and the Breast and Ovarian CFRs are:

- Philadelphia Familial Breast Cancer Registry collects a great deal of clinical and epidemiological data from both patients and their families. It also collects longitudinal data from registry participants.
- The steering committee is the official governing body of the Breast and Ovarian CFRs. This committee is responsible for developing the core protocols for biospecimen collection, the core instruments for the collection of epidemiological and clinical data, and policies and procedures.
- The Breast and Ovarian CFRs also have an advisory board, which is an independent, multidisciplinary panel of senior cancer researchers that evaluates researcher requests for use of the

registries' resources. This committee makes recommendations on research priorities to the steering committee, which ratifies the recommendations based on the feasibility of providing the requested resources.

- The Breast and Ovarian CFRs also have a publications working group that oversees all issues associated with publications.
- The Informatics Center at the University of California at Irvine serves as a centralized data resource for the six member registries. It designed the bioinformatics system, provides guidelines for data standardization and specimen anonymization, and implements network and database security, such as password protection, encryption, and firewalls.

National Heart, Blood, and Lung Institute

NHLBI maintains primarily blood and some tissue specimens as part of several studies. Tissue is distributed to government institutions and academic researchers. The bioinformatics system at the storage repository is used for repository management only, but the tissue data bioinformatics systems maintained by the Data Coordinating Center are capable of sophisticated statistical analysis. Privacy, ethical, and consent issues are determined by the study protocol, but they are carefully overseen by IRBs in all cases, and by specific committees for each study. The specimens and intellectual property belong to NHLBI. For the LAM (Lymphangioleiomyomatosis) study, marketing is primarily done through word of mouth because of the small target population; however, there is also some outreach at scientific meetings. Other relevant findings for NHLBI are:

- The LAM Registry has a specific plan for recruiting tissue sources. The LAM Registry's close contacts with medical facilities associated with the registry and trained staff are good models for standardization. In addition, the LAM Registry has developed a consent template that participating centers can reformat according to the needs of their institution.
- BBI Biotech has outstanding quality control, testing, and standardization for shipping, data entry, and specimen storage.

Armed Forces Institute of Pathology National Pathology Repository

AFIP is a secondary referral center for expert pathology diagnostics. Most of the tissue maintained by AFIP is used internally or in collaboration with internal pathologists and other researchers. The bioinformatics system is designed to manage large volumes of tissue data. It tracks the collection and distribution of samples but does not track clinical outcomes or outside research using the samples. The repository is not involved in consent issues that arise at the time of the surgery. IRB and tissue utilization committees deal with privacy and ethical issues related to tissue use and distribution. In addition to advertising at national meetings, AFIP produces a newsletter six times a year that has a broad distribution to 17,000 pathologists, 5,000 of whom are outside the United States. AFIP also produces both an annual report and an annual research progress report. AFIP is currently developing a new business and marketing plan. Other findings of significance are:

- AFIP has the single largest and most comprehensive collection of pathology material in the world. The sheer magnitude (more than 90 million specimens) and age (dating back to 1864) of AFIP's specimen collection, as well as the wealth of information that has been collected about the specimens at AFIP, make these specimens valuable as historical controls and for ascertaining changes over time.
- AFIP has good quality control and standardization given the variety of specimens it receives. Each specimen is checked against its associated data and identification number by three different people. In addition, there is a standard protocol for the processing and storage of each specimen.
- AFIP has the capability to provide samples accompanied by a wide array of information.

Duke University Breast SPORE

Duke University, which operates one of the NCI-funded SPOREs for breast cancer research, is funded through a Specialized Center Grant (P50) from NCI. Duke University Breast SPORE collects specimens from patients at the Duke medical facility. It collects specimens for banking, as well as prospectively based upon specific research needs. The majority of its specimens (80 percent) are used for academic research. A smaller portion (20 percent) is used for government research. The Duke University Breast SPORE bioinformatics system is used primarily to catalog and track specimens in the repository; it was not designed for highly advanced searches. Duke University Breast SPORE trains its personnel in obtaining informed consent. It does not require IRB approval from outside requesters of unlinked (i.e., anonymized) samples, nor does it have a claim on intellectual property rights for samples it provides to others, although it does maintain such rights on any collaborative research in which it engages. Duke University Breast SPORE does not market itself. A novel procedure developed at Duke University Breast SPORE is as follows:

- Duke University Breast SPORE developed a new protocol to collect breast tissue because of increased difficulty obtaining sizable amounts of tissue given more focused breast surgeries (e.g., small lumpectomies). It developed a method of extracting a core from limited resection (e.g., lumpectomy) specimens without affecting the diagnostic ability of surgical pathologists.

Mayo Clinic Prostate SPORE

Mayo Clinic Prostate SPORE, which is funded through a Specialized Center Grant (P50) from NCI, performs both prospective tissue collection and banking. It collects tissue from two Mayo hospitals and distributes 90 to 95 percent of that tissue to Mayo researchers. It uses a Microsoft Access® database that includes scanned H&E stained slides to manage the repository. The Access® database can be cross-referenced with a clinical database. Full informed consent for the collection of tissue is obtained within 24 hours after surgery, and full IRB approval is required from researchers who request tissue. For tissue to be released outside of Mayo Clinic Prostate SPORE, a materials transfer agreement needs to be completed. Mayo Clinic Prostate SPORE does not perform any marketing of its repository. Other interesting findings are:

- Mayo Clinic Prostate SPORE does not provide any testing or preparation of tissue. However, because it is centrally located near other "core" facilities, if a researcher requests DNA or RNA preparations, it works with the researcher and the other core facilities to provide that service.
- Mayo Clinic Prostate SPORE collects longitudinal data and bodily fluids on all patients getting a radical prostatectomy. This includes pre-operative, operative, and follow-up data obtained at clinical visits, through questionnaires, and through the referring physician, if necessary. The Mayo SPORE also collects serum and urine from prostate patients at 3- to 6-month intervals.

University of Alabama at Birmingham Breast and Ovarian SPOREs
The UAB Breast and Ovarian SPOREs are funded through Specialized Center Grants (P50s) from NCI. Both SPOREs complement ongoing programs at the UAB Comprehensive Cancer Center. In addition to the Breast and Ovarian SPOREs, UAB has a Brain SPORE and a new Pancreas SPORE. It is also one of the biomarker validation laboratories for EDRN and serves as the Southern Division of CHTN. The SPOREs are primarily involved in tissue banking for future use once clinical outcomes data become available. The bioinformatics system used by the SPOREs is specifically for repository management purposes. Biospecimens are collected with specific informed consent for donation, and researchers are required to have IRB approval for research that uses the SPOREs' resources. The SPOREs have no intellectual property position. Researchers sign an agreement to use the SPOREs' resources and accept liability for the use of the resources in this agreement. The SPOREs only market their resources internally at UAB through conferences. Other findings of interest are:

- The UAB Breast and Ovarian SPOREs collect high-quality tissue and associated data. They are able to collect some tissues from most patients within 15 minutes of availability from the operating room. They utilize patient questionnaires in association with a bioinformatics facility to collect demographic and medical history, as well as familial history of cancer and other information. They also collect clinical outcomes data through the tumor registry.

- UAB Breast SPORE has collected tissue from approximately 700 breast cancers and 1,000 uninvolved breasts, and UAB Ovarian SPORE has collected tissue from approximately 500 ovarian cancers and 1,000 uninvolved ovaries. However, they have not begun distributing many samples from these collections, because they are allowing time for the resource to mature—that is, they are trying to minimize use until there are enough longitudinal data for follow-up. The UAB SPOREs have found that it usually takes about four to five years for a tissue collection to "mature" to the point that there are enough follow-up data to be useful.

University of Pittsburgh Health Sciences Tissue Bank

University of Pittsburgh HSTB was established in 1991. It performs both prospective tissue collection and banking of resected tumors from the prostate, gastrointestinal tract, lung, liver, breast, head and neck, gynecological sites, muscle, and skin. University of Pittsburgh HSTB distributes over 90 percent of its tissue to UPMC researchers. Its OSD integration engine automatically integrates the tissue bank inventory system, the pathology report, and the cancer registry system. It also includes results from DNA microarray experiments and is both minable and Web based. The repository is primarily publicly funded. It has IRB approval to collect tissue, and the tissue sources are consented prior to and separate from the surgery. Researchers requesting samples are required to have IRB approval of their research. Intellectual property rights for research on the tissue belong to the institutions performing the research (primarily UPMC). University of Pittsburgh HSTB advertises by word of mouth, Web sites, an exhibit at an annual meeting of cancer researchers, and an annual meeting on pathology informatics that it hosts in Pittsburgh. Other findings of interest at University of Pittsburgh HSTB are:

- The University of Pittsburgh HSTB tissue collection includes a wide variety of tissue: cancerous tissue, non-diseased matching adjacent tissue, metastatic tumore (through the Warm Autopsy Program, from patients who consent before passing away), normal tissue from patients who have donated their organs for transplant and research, and blood products.
- The University of Pittsburgh HSTB OSD integration engine integrates multiple data systems. It automatically pulls de-identified information from the surgical pathology report, includes longitudinal and outcomes data from the cancer registry, and includes genomic data. All of this is searchable via the Web.
- The University of Pittsburgh HSTB OSD integration engine is the basis for the Pennsylvania Cancer Alliance Bioinformatics Consortium, a partnership comprising six institutes in Pennsylvania that are sharing tissue resources and data to enhance translational and clinical cancer research. The consortium is developing a statewide data model for bioinformatics and a statewide repository of serum and tissue specimens.
- University of Pittsburgh HSTB stores tissues in the vapor phase of liquid nitrogen at $-134°C$ to $-170°C$, which, according to UPMC researchers, maintains the genomic integrity better than storage at $-80°C$ does.
- University of Pittsburgh Research Informatics (as well as the information technology group) is integrated with the scientists, making the system very user friendly and information friendly. It is in constant support of growth and integration.

Ardais

Ardais is a private company that began operations in 1999. The company grew out of a mutual interest between researchers at Duke Medical Center and Ardais founders to develop a tissue/data banking resource for Duke and the greater research community. Ardais performs standardized collection and banking of tissues and distributes its tissue specimens to the four contributing institutes, other academic researchers, and private industry. The Ardais bioinformatics system, BIGR™, includes pathology data, is used for repository management, and is searchable by researchers requesting tissue. Ardais is primarily privately funded. Informed consent from tissue sources is obtained specifically for the collection of tissue specimens for research purposes. The company has IRB approval to collect tissues, and IRB approval—either from the requester's IRB or the Ardais IRB—is required to request tissues. Ardais does not have a formal intellectual property policy. Marketing takes place through scientific meetings, word of mouth, and a seminar series Ardais sponsors on clinical genomics. Other relevant findings at Ardais are:

- Ardais's tissue procurement system, with pathology assistants working in each hospital, ensures that Ardais gets as many tissue samples as possible.
- Ardais's quality assurance system is state of the art. All specimens are bar coded and scanned. Inventory lists, including incoming specimens, samples being used for quality assurance, and outgoing samples, are computerized. All personnel working with tissue use scanning guns when adding information to the BIGR™ database for the tissue.
- Ardais's laboratory offers a wide variety of services with its tissue (DNA/RNA/protein preparations, tissue microassay, laser capture microdissection, and immunohistochemistry) and is constantly working on developing new services.
- Ardais's information technology group is well integrated with the scientists, making the BIGR™ system user and information friendly.

Genomics Collaborative Inc.

GCI was established in 1998, primarily as a for-profit private biotechnology research company. GCI has a fee-for-service side (~65 percent of its business) that works primarily with the pharmaceutical industry to design and collect specimens for drug development. It also participates in larger collaborative research programs with pharmaceutical companies, biotech companies, and academic and government institutions. The GCI bioinformatics system serves as a repository management tool and as a database of research results.

GCI trains coordinators to obtain informed consent from tissue sources. Tissue specimens are collected with identifiable information, but the link between the specimen and the patient is permanently destroyed. For blood and serum specimens, the link between the specimen and the patient is kept by a third party. The intellectual property rights belong to the customer on the fee-for-service side and are shared among collaborators on the research side. GCI engages in a minimal amount of marketing at conferences and through some journals. Other findings of interest at GCI are:

- GCI has created an impressive bioinformatics system (the Laboratory Information Management System, or LIMS) that is a state-of-the-art "cradle to grave" sample and data tracking system.
- GCI has multiple quality assurance procedures in place (e.g., every tube and slide in the collection kit has the same bar code, and additional bar code stickers are supplied to be attached to any accompanying paperwork). Bar codes on all the specimens are scanned once they arrive at GCI, and laboratory technicians check for any inconsistencies.
- GCI employs two pathologists that review every specimen collection kit that arrives. The pathologists are able to check for the quality of specimens collected and the accuracy of their preparation. The pathologists verify the diagnosis and add any further annotation deemed necessary.
- GCI follows strict ethical standards. It created a bioethics advisory board that includes nationally recognized bioethics experts. The board helped GCI develop its operating procedures and meets four times a year to review procedures and recommend any necessary adjustments. GCI uses a third-party system for patient information that allows for longitudinal patient follow-up while maintaining several firewalls of protection for patient identity.

Best Practices

The sequencing of the human genome and recent advances in genomic and proteomic research have improved the understanding of the biology of cancer and have resulted in new ways to prevent, diagnose, and treat cancer. The use of biospecimens has been key to the discovery of many of these advances in cancer care.

These valuable biospecimens and associated data are collected and stored at hundreds of tissue repositories in the United States. However, there are currently no national standards in place for tissue repositories that collect and store specimens for use in research.[1] Therefore, the way one repository collects, processes, and stores its specimens may be very different from that of another repository, which may complicate comparisons of research results obtained using biospecimens from different repositories. The quality and the extent of clinical information collected with the specimens also vary from repository to repository. In addition, the type of informed consent obtained from many of the tissue sources of these specimens is not sufficiently robust to allow the use of these specimens in research that requires long-term follow-up of clinically relevant data. Furthermore, once samples are distributed to researchers, most repositories do not require those researchers to report research results back to the repository, and even fewer repositories enter those research results into their bioinformatics systems and make them available to the broader research community.

The NBN Design Team recognized the limitations of existing repositories and concluded that the development of a nationally coordinated, standardized, high-quality tissue resource and data bank

---

[1] Professional societies, such as the International Society for Biological and Environmental Repositories (ISBER) and the National Committee for Clinical Laboratory Standards (NCCLS), have recognized the need for standardization and are developing guidance for establishing and operating biospecimen repositories. ISBER is creating a set of Best Practices for Repositories to provide repository professionals with guidance on repository activities. The NCCLS guidelines will cover all health care institutions and clinics that collect human tissue for research purposes, and will provide standards for addressing all issues associated with the collection of human tissue to support biomedical research, including the ethical, legislative, and legal concerns.

was necessary for the nation to ultimately realize the promise of genomics and proteomics for preventing and curing cancer and other diseases. The NBN Design Team envisioned a network of geographically dispersed tissue repositories to collect, process, store, and distribute appropriately consented diseased and normal tissue and other biological specimens with associated clinical data supported and coordinated by an accessible, user-friendly bioinformatics system networked across the country. The biospecimens would be collected, processed, annotated, stored, and distributed in a highly standardized manner to minimize experimental variability and accelerate scientific progress. The NBN would also contain research data submitted by investigators who use NBN samples.

Based on an evaluation of existing human tissue resources at twelve tissue repositories, RAND found best practices that the NBN Design Team and the TAWG may want to consider as they implement their plan for the NBN. The following sections summarize the combination of best practices required to build a robust resource for genomics- and proteomics-based research.

Best Practices for Biospecimen Collection, Processing, Annotation, Storage, and Distribution

The network of geographically dispersed tissue repositories to collect, process, annotate, store, and distribute tissue envisioned by the NBN Design Team is very similar to how some of the repositories evaluated for this study are set up. CHTN, EDRN, the Breast and Ovarian CFRs (of which Philadelphia Familial Breast Cancer Registry is a member), and University of Pittsburgh HSTB are all variations of the model of a network of geographically dispersed tissue repositories with decentralized collection, storage, and distribution. NHLBI, AFIP, Ardais, and GCI have a decentralized collection model but maintain storage and distribution of samples at one physical location. TARP also has a decentralized collection model with its bioinformatics system and storage maintained at one physical location, but TARP tissue microarrays are distributed to users by CHTN Eastern Division. In contrast, Duke University Breast SPORE, Mayo Clinic Prostate SPORE, and the UAB Breast and Ovarian SPOREs have centralized collection, storage, and distribution. Best practices in the areas of biospecimen collection, processing, annotation, storage, and distribution were observed at all of these repositories.

Best Practices for Biospecimen Collection. Several repositories have established networks of collection sites at academic medical centers and community hospitals to obtain the number and variety of high-quality samples and associated data needed by researchers. Repositories are also collecting tissue from ethnically diverse populations of all ages and from countries other than the United States to ensure the diversity of tissues available for research purposes. In addition to collecting tissues from a broad range of diseases, including cancer, diabetes, and vascular, inflammatory, and metabolic diseases, repositories are collecting non-diseased matching adjacent tissue, normal tissue (from autopsy, organ donation, or patients undergoing surgery for a different condition), and blood and blood components for comparison to diseased tissue. These **best practices** for biospecimen collection will increase the number and variety of high-quality samples with appropriate normal controls that are demographically representative of the population. (For details on best practices for biospecimen collection practiced by each repository see Table 10.2.)

All of the repositories utilize pathologists to determine what tissue is necessary for pathologic diagnosis and what is excess and available to give to the repository for storage and research use. The pathologist takes what is necessary for patient treatment and diagnosis and immediately gives the remainder to trained repository personnel who begin the sample preservation protocol. At all of the repositories, patient care and the pathological diagnosis have absolute priority over the use of any specimen in research. The prioritization of patient diagnosis over collection of specimens for research purposes and the use of pathologists to initially procure the portion of the specimen destined for the repository are **best practices** that will ensure that patient care is not compromised and that patients continue to donate biospecimens.

Table 10.2
Best Practices for Biospecimen Collection

Biospecimen Collection	CHTN	TARP	EDRN	Philadelphia Familial BCR	NHLBI/BBI	AFIP	Duke University Breast SPORE	Mayo Clinic Prostate SPORE	UAB Breast & Ovarian SPOREs	Univ. of Pittsburgh HSTB	Ardais	GCI
Collect from ethnically and geographically diverse populations of all ages	✔	✔	✔	✗		✔	✗	✗	✗	✗	✗	✗
Draw from large network of academic and community medical centers	✔	✔	✔	✔		✔					✗	✔
Pathologist determines proportion of specimen needed for diagnosis	✔	✔	✔	✔	✔	✔	✔	✔	✔	✔	✔	✔
Standardized, monitored shipping procedures with a tracking system	✔	✔[a]	✗	[b]	✔[c]						✔	✔
Specimen QA through H&E analysis, pathologist review, and integrity check	✔	✔		✔			✗	✔	✔	✔	✔	✔
Scannable bar codes to track specimens	✗	✗[d]	✗				✔			✗[d]	✔	✔
SOPs for specimen collection	✔	✔	✔					✔	✔	✔	✔	✔
Train collection personnel using standard protocols	✔	✔[a]	✗					✔	✔	✔	✔	✔
Close contact with collection site personnel to ensure standards	✔	✔[a]	✗						✔	✔	✔	✔

NOTE: ✔ = repository fully incorporates this best practice; ✗ = repository incorporates some aspects of this best practice.
[a] CHTN Eastern Division collects the specimens used to make the TARP microarrays and distributes the microarrays.
[b] Philadelphia Familial Breast Cancer Registry uses the Coriell Cell Repositories to store its specimens.
[c] NHLBI uses BBI to store specimens for the LAM and several other studies.
[d] TARP and University of Pittsburgh HSTB are converting to a bar-code system.

Most of the repositories utilize repository personnel or collection-site personnel (pathology assistants, tissue technicians, histotechnologists) who are specifically trained by the repository to collect and process biospecimens. In addition, many of the repositories have developed their own SOPs for biospecimen collection and preparation that are established uniformly at all collecting sites. Repository-trained personnel are provided with these standardized protocols to follow for the collection and processing of biospecimens. In addition, some repositories use standardized collection kits that are given to all sites for the collection and processing of biospecimens. Using repository-trained personnel for the collection and processing of biospecimens, and developing SOPs and providing standard collection and processing equipment for those personnel to use are **best practices** that will promote standardized tissue collection and processing.

Some of the repositories employ a bar-coding system to track every specimen and its associated information from the time of collection through the time of distribution. Each specimen vial, storage box, and associated pathology report is bar coded and logged into the bioinformatics system. The use of scannable bar codes or other electronic technology to track biospecimens and associated information throughout their lifetime at the repository is a **best practice**.

Best Practices for Biospecimen Processing and Annotation. At most of the repositories, pathologists are responsible for verification and evaluation of biospecimens collected by the repository. The pathologist confirms the identity and diagnosis of the specimen by matching the tissue received with the pathology report and other documents provided and reviewing an H&E stained slide made from each specimen. Results and annotations gathered from tests performed on the specimens upon arrival and throughout the life of the specimen at the repository are linked to the specimens at all repositories evaluated for this study. At some repositories, any additional information about the specimen obtained through the quality control histopathologic examination is provided to researchers, and digital images of stained slides are posted to the database for examination by researchers. The verification and evaluation by a pathologist of biospecimens collected by the repository is a **best practice** to ensure that high-quality specimens are procured. (For details on best practices for biospecimen processing and annotation practiced by each repository see Table 10.3.)

Best practices for data collection depend on the mission of the repository. Collections of biospecimens used primarily by basic researchers may only require minimal associated clinical data, such as demographic data and pathology reports. Biospecimens collected for translational research (e.g., target identification or validation) may require more in-depth associated clinical data, such as medical and family histories, treatment, and clinical outcomes data. No matter what the requirements for the amount of associated data are, certain best practices are applicable. Collecting consistent and high-quality data associated with biospecimens and employing a standardized set of common data elements that are collected with every biospecimen are **best practices**. In addition to collecting basic demographic and pathologic data, some repositories collect extensive data on family history, medical history, lifestyle and diet history, treatment, and clinical outcomes. Collecting complete data on all elements in a minimal data set designed to fulfill the mission of the repository and meet the needs of its users is a **best practice.**

The repositories that collect longitudinal data do so through annual questionnaires or tumor registries or directly from hospital medical records. Tissue sources are informed during the consent process that they will be asked to fill out a questionnaire or that information from their medical records will be obtained in the future. Each of these methods has its limitations. Annual questionnaires sent to tissue sources rely on self-reporting by the tissue source. Tumor registries and hospitals routinely lose track of tissue sources due to high rates of mobility of some patients. The ability to effectively collect and store longitudinal data is a **best practice.**

Table 10.3
Best Practices for Biospecimen Processing and Annotation

Biospecimen Processing and Annotation	CHTN	TARP	EDRN	Philadelphia Familial BCR	NHLBI/BBI	AFIP	Duke University Breast SPORE	Mayo Clinic Prostate SPORE	UAB Breast & Ovarian SPOREs	Univ. of Pittsburgh HSTB	Ardais	GCI
Procure and process specimens for storage within one hour post-excision using detailed, standardized protocols	✗		✔				✗	✗	✗	✔	✔	✔
Use pathologists to verify and evaluate biospecimens	✔	✔		✔			✔	✔	✔	✔	✔	✔
Link all assay/test results and relevant annotation to specimens and provide information to researchers	✔	✔	✔	✔	✔[a]	✔		✔	✔	✔	✔	✔
Provide information/annotation obtained during QC of specimen in a database for researchers to access	✗		✔					✔	✗	✔	✔	
Use common data elements for standardized data collection	✔	✔	✔	✔				✔		✔	✔	✔
Collect complete data on all elements of a minimal data set to meet user needs	✗		✗	✔	✗		✗	✗	✔	✗	✗	✔
Collect and store longitudinal data	✗	✗	✔	✔	✔	✗	✔	✔	✔	✔	✗	✗
Ensure the accuracy of data entry through the use of standardized terminology and computer data-entry forms	✔								✔	✔	✔	✔
Implement independent checks of data	✔	✔[a]	✔	✔	✔	✔		✗	✗	✔	✔	✔

NOTE: ✔ = repository fully incorporates this best practice; ✗ = repository incorporates some aspects of this best practice.
[a] Practices followed by NHLBI for the LAM study.

Once data are collected, they must be entered into the repository's bioinformatics system. Some of the repositories have developed procedures for ensuring accurate data entry. Some collect common data elements and use standardized terminology for data collection procedures, which allows for the creation of data-entry forms complete with drop-down menus and other features that minimize the error introduced while typing information into forms. Others use automated methods, such as parsing techniques, to flag discrepancies and keep records of when error tracking and reconciliation are done. Ensuring the accuracy of data entry through the use of standardized terminology and computer data-entry forms (e.g., drop-down menus) whenever possible is a **best practice**.

Best Practices for Biospecimen Storage and Distribution. Several repositories have developed standards for storage depending on tissue type and preservation condition (e.g., snap frozen, paraffin embedded, tissue microarray). Snap-frozen specimens are commonly stored at −80°C in mechanical freezers or in liquid nitrogen. Paraffin-embedded tissue and tissue microarrays are stored at room temperature under conditions that will protect them from melting or other damage. However, there is no consensus on the optimum storage conditions for specimens. Some repositories use bar-coded inventory systems to track specimen location. Establishing standard operating procedures for biospecimen storage and using a bar-coding inventory system are **best practices** for ensuring that specimens are stored appropriately and are accessible for distribution when necessary. (For details on best practices for biospecimen storage and distribution practiced by each repository see Table 10.4.)

Once specimens are placed in storage, it is necessary to monitor storage conditions and maintain equipment in good working order. Most repositories utilize a monitored central alarm system, have backup generators or liquid nitrogen backup, and maintain enough empty freezer space to allow for quick transfer of specimens from malfunctioning freezers. Some repositories have developed standard operating procedures specifically for the daily, weekly, monthly, and yearly maintenance procedures, and have maintenance agreements

Table 10.4
Best Practices for Biospecimen Storage and Distribution

Biospecimen Storage and Distribution	CHTN	TARP	EDRN	Philadelphia Familial BCR	NHLBI/BBI	AFIP	Duke University Breast SPORE	Mayo Clinic Prostate SPORE	UAB Breast & Ovarian SPOREs	Univ. of Pittsburgh HSTB	Ardais	GCI
Collect non-diseased matching adjacent tissue; normal tissue and blood/serum specimens	✔	✔	✗				✗	✗	✗	✗	✗	✔
Develop standards for storage depending on tissue type and storage condition[a]	✗	✗	✗	✔[b]	✔[c]	✔	✗	✔	✗	✗	✗	✔
Monitor specimens around the clock, perform, weekly maintenance and annual quality checks of freezers, and use freezer backup procedures[d]	✔		✗	✔[b]	✔[c]		✗	✗	✗	✔	✔	✔
Use multiple storage sites (on or off site)	✔		✗	✔[b]						✗		✔
Periodically audit, inventory, and certify location, identity, and quality of specimens	✔		✗	✔[b]	✔[c]				✗	✔	✔	✔

NOTE: ✔ = repository fully incorporates this best practice; ✗ = repository incorporates some aspects of this best practice.
[a]There does not appear to be an accepted industry standard for storing frozen tissue.
[b]Coriell Cell Repositories, which is used by Philadelphia Familial BCR to store its specimens, incorporates these best practices.
[c]BBI Biotech, which is used by NHLBI to store specimens from several studies, incorporates these best practices.
[d]See Chapter Three for a list of effective procedures.

with professional periodic maintenance. Some repositories even utilize multiple storage locations, which can be on site (i.e., specimens are divided between two or more freezers), on site and offsite, or in a network of storage facilities. Standard operating procedures for freezer maintenance, adequate backup equipment, and redundancy in storage location are **best practices** to ensure that specimens are stored and maintained at the necessary temperature and condition and that specimen integrity is not compromised.

Some repositories do periodic checks of specimen integrity (e.g., examining new histology slides and testing RNA integrity), while others review and verify pathology reports to ensure that the biospecimen fulfills the researcher's request. Utilizing standardized storage techniques and periodically auditing, inventorying, and certifying the location, identity, and quality of specimens are **best practices** that will ensure the quality and integrity of samples sent to researchers.

Some repositories use standardized and carefully monitored shipping procedures that are integrated with the repository's bioinformatics system to track all shipments in and out of the repository. Biospecimens sent to the repository from remote/satellite sites and samples sent from the repository to researchers are tracked using a bar-coded inventory system. Using standardized and carefully monitored shipping procedures with systems to track all shipments and expected receipts is a **best practice**.

Specimen distribution practices clearly depend on the mission of the repository. If the mission is to provide tissue samples to as broad a researcher base as possible based on the quality of the proposed research, then biospecimen distribution policies should be established to fulfill this mission. If the mission is clearly defined and the repository evaluates its ability to meet its goals, and changes policies, procedures, and practices when it is not meeting its goals, then this is a **best practice**.

Quality Assurance and Standardization of Biospecimen Collection, Processing, Annotation, Storage, and Distribution. Quality assurance is fundamental to the successful operation of any repository that collects, processes, annotates, stores, and distributes biospecimens for research purposes. The use of standardized protocols for collection, storage, processing, and distribution of specimens, and common data elements for the annotation of specimens at each of the individual network participant locations makes comparative research across participating institutions possible and is a **best practice**.

To ensure that the collection, processing, annotation, storage, and distribution of biospecimens occur at consistently high levels of quality, it is necessary to have a multitiered, fully integrated system of quality assurance (including quality control) and standard operating procedures. Quality assurance starts with training of personnel before biospecimens are ever collected and includes everything up through considering researcher feedback on sample quality. Some of the best practices of quality assurance and standardization for biospecimen collection, processing, annotation, storage, and distribution observed at the repositories evaluated for this study are:

- Train all personnel who are involved in the collection, processing, annotation, storage, and distribution of tissue.
- Standardize collection, processing, annotation, storage, and distribution protocols to ensure the highest quality samples and comparability of research results.
- Perform appropriate quality control testing on each specimen, such as histopathology (H&E), immunohistochemistry, testing for DNA/RNA integrity, or other quality control testing as appropriate.
- Bar code all specimens and data so it is easy both to match the specimen with the pathology report and other associated data and to locate the specimen in the storage facility.
- Use researcher feedback about sample quality to re-examine quality control procedures.

Best Practices for Bioinformatics

The NBN Design Team noted that a bioinformatics system should be standardized, scalable and secure, and appropriate for program management, data aggregation, tissue acquisition and management, and data analysis. These characteristics were observed to varying degrees in the bioinformatics systems of the repositories evaluated. All of the repositories used their bioinformatics systems for repository management; however, very few of the repositories fed research results back into the database, and none of the repositories shared its data publicly. (For details on best practices for bioinformatics practiced by each repository see Table 10.5.)

The bioinformatics systems at the repositories ranged from simple Microsoft Access® databases to internally developed proprietary systems. Most repositories established close ties among the bioinformatics system developers, the researchers, the data managers, and repository management. This is a **best practice** that allows the bioinformatics system to be designed so that it is responsive to the needs of multiple types of users.

Table 10.5
Best Practices for Bioinformatics

Bioinformatics	CHTN	TARP	EDRN	Philadelphia Familial BCR	NHLBI/BBI	AFIP	Duke University Breast SPORE	Mayo Clinic Prostate SPORE	UAB Breast & Ovarian SPOREs	Univ. of Pittsburgh HSTB	Ardais	GCI
Maintain close relationship with system developers, researchers, data managers, and repository managers	✔	✔	✔	✔	✔	✔		✔	✔	✔	✔	✔
Use automated data extraction or multiple checks/standardized language in bioinformatics system	✔				✔	✔			✕	✔	✔	✔
Feed research results back into system for access by researchers				✔			✕	✕		✔		✕[a]
Employ a searchable and minable Web-based system	✕	✕	✕	✔	✕				✕	✔	✔	✕
Provide extensive network security and access control	✔	✔	✔	✔	✔	✔	✔	✔	✔	✔	✔	✔

NOTE: ✔ = repository fully incorporates this best practice; ✕ = repository incorporates some aspects of this best practice.
[a]Research results for GCI collaborative studies are fed back into GCI's bioinformatics system; research results from samples distributed via fee-for-service are not.

Several repositories use a standardized language to categorize and describe biospecimens and enter data into the bioinformatics system. The repositories were also using various techniques to ensure the accuracy of the data entered into the database. Some of the sites manually double or triple check the data entered into their systems using independent technicians or researchers; other sites rely on automated software or random or requested checks to validate their data. In addition, some of the databases were set up to allow the repository's bioinformatics system to interface with the medical informatics system located at the collection site to automatically extract data. Using standardized language to categorize and describe biospecimens and enter data into the bioinformatics system is a **best practice** that will allow comparison of biospecimen characteristics among collection sites. In addition, using either an automated data extraction system or multiple checks of data entry is a **best practice** to ensure accuracy of the data in the bioinformatics system.

Only a few of the repositories currently feed data from research performed with their samples back into the repository data system, and fewer still collect genomics or proteomics data. A **best practice** for bioinformatics systems is feeding standard research results and genomics and proteomics results back into the system for other researchers to access.

All of the bioinformatics systems are searchable, and many databases are Web based. In some cases, researchers have access to some data; in others, data coordinating centers or other data managers retain sole access. A few of the bioinformatics systems were specifically created to allow data mining and advanced statistical analysis. A bioinformatics system that is searchable and minable via varying levels of Web-based access for different individuals (including repository personnel, researchers, patients, and the public) is a **best practice**.

Most of the repositories exercise access control to their data, allowing researchers, physicians, and others to access limited data while maintaining strict control over the ability to manipulate the data. All of the repositories use both cyber and physical means to protect the data. Network security systems and access control are **best practices** to ensure that privacy is protected and that the bioinformatics system is secure.

Best Practices for Consumer/User Needs

A repository is only successful if it is meeting its users' needs. This involves continual self-assessment and re-evaluation. However, meeting user needs means different things to each repository and depends on the repository's design, its customer profile, and its product offerings. Assessing the needs of researchers, tracking the numbers and types of tissue samples distributed, and using this information to quickly change collection priorities to match customer demand is a **best practice**. (For details on best practices for consumer/user needs practiced by each repository see Table 10.6.)

The review and prioritization system for tissue distribution at the repositories generally falls into one of four general categories: (1) first come, first served; (2) priority to members of the network, collaborators, and/or contributors to the repository; (3) prioritization based on merit review of research proposals; or (4) prioritization based on a set policy of the repository. Some of the repositories use a tissue utilization committee to prioritize tissue distribution, especially for requests for large amounts of tissue and rare tissue. A few of the repositories also have policies to control the distribution of the last sample of a particular specimen and to prevent the control of an entire specimen or type of specimen by one researcher. **Best practices** to ensure equitable distribution of tissue to a large group of researchers include the use of a tissue utilization committee to prioritize tissue distribution based on merit review of researcher proposals, and policies to control the distribution of rare specimens, to control the last sample of a particular specimen, and to prevent the monopolization of an entire specimen or type of specimen by one researcher.

At some repositories, researchers at institutions that are collection sites for the repositories receive some level of priority over other researchers for tissue distribution. Giving priority to researchers at collecting institutions is a **best practice** that leads to increased support for the resource and higher investment in the quality of the specimens collected.

Table 10.6
Best Practices for Consumer/User Needs

Consumer/User Needs	CHTN	TARP	EDRN	Philadelphia Familial BCR	NHLBI/BBI	AFIP	Duke University Breast SPORE	Mayo Clinic Prostate SPORE	UAB Breast & Ovarian SPOREs	Univ. of Pittsburgh HSTB	Ardais	GCI
Give priority to researchers at collecting institutions	X		✔				✔	✔	✔	✔	✔	✔
Base prioritization on merit review using tissue utilization committee and standardized criteria			✔	✔		✔		✔	✔	✔	X	✔
Have policies to prevent last sample distribution and researcher monopolization of samples	✔	✔		✔	✔			✔	✔	✔	✔	
Directly solicit researcher feedback on particular samples/shipment	✔	✔		✔					X	✔	✔	✔
Evaluate repository performance through committees/review groups	✔		✔	✔					✔	✔	✔	✔
Regularly assess and change in response to researcher needs	✔	✔ᵃ								✔	✔	✔

NOTE: ✔ = repository fully incorporates this best practice; X = repository incorporates some aspects of this best practice.
ᵃConsumer feedback to TARP is coordinated through CHTN.

Committees or review groups in which both providers and consumers are able to provide input on the usefulness of the repository resources are valuable in evaluating how well the repository is meeting user needs. In addition, solicitation of direct researcher feedback on the quality of samples received helps to identify systemic problems, inconsistencies, or problems with specimens in the repository or specimens being collected in a certain way or from a certain collection site. These **best practices** enable repositories to improve specimen quality and be responsive to researcher needs.

Best Practices for Business Plan and Operations

The repositories evaluated for this study are funded primarily by the federal government or the private sector and are located at federal agencies, academic institutions, and private companies. Different business models are represented among the repositories evaluated, including tissue banking versus prospective collection and distribution, networks versus individual sites, and centralized versus decentralized collection, storage, and bioinformatics systems. Establishing a network of collection sites at academic medical centers and community hospitals to perform a combination of banking to collect and maintain a ready supply of tissue and prospective collection to meet researcher needs is a **best practice**. (For details on best practices for business plan and operations practiced by each repository see Table 10.7.)

Many of those interviewed indicated that when first beginning discussions with a medical facility about its becoming a participating collection site, it was more productive to talk with the pathologists and surgeons rather than the administrators. Ultimately, it is necessary to establish good working relationships with all levels of collection site staff. Establishing and maintaining close working relationships with surgeons, pathologists, nurses, and other relevant staff at the collection sites is a **best practice**.

Most repositories did not know the cost to collect, process, store, and distribute samples, and the industry repositories declined to provide cost information. The few repositories that could provide cost estimates gave costs of between $60 and $150 per sample. Part of this price differential depends on the amount of clinical information accompanying the biospecimen—the more information, the higher the cost of collecting the tissue. Likewise, only a few repositories provided information about the cost of samples to researchers. At these repositories, the price of samples ranged from free of charge to $200. Tissue microarrays ranged in price from $40 for academic researchers to $120 for industry researchers. Accurately determining the actual

Table 10.7
Best Practices for Business Plan and Operations

Business Plan and Operations	CHTN	TARP	EDRN	Philadelphia Familial BCR	NHLBI/BBI	AFIP	Duke University Breast SPORE	Mayo Clinic Prostate SPORE	UAB Breast & Ovarian SPOREs	Univ. of Pittsburgh HSTB	Ardais	GCI
Establish and maintain close relationships with all relevant staff at collection sites	✔								✔	✔	✔	✔
Combine banking and prospective tissue collection	✔	✔	✔				✔	✔		✔	✔	✔
Accurately determine costs of all stages of repository operation to financially sustain repository	✔	✔				✗			✔	✗	✔[a]	✗[a]
Continually assess and incorporate new technologies	✔	✔	✗	✗	✗	✗	✔	✗	✗	✔	✔	✔
Require acknowledgment of repository in publications and provide specific language with which to do so	✔	✔	✔	✔		✔			✗	✔		

NOTE: ✔ = repository fully incorporates this best practice; ✗ = repository incorporates some aspects of this best practice.
[a] Ardais and GCI declined to share the costs of repository operations. However, both repositories reported that they have accurately determined the costs of repository operation to financially sustain the repository.

costs of collecting, processing, storing, and distributing tissue samples to researchers, and operating on a cost recovery basis to financially sustain the repository is a **best practice**.

All the repositories that were evaluated claimed to constantly be on the lookout for new technologies that would improve their processes. Some have regular meetings with staff to brainstorm the issue; others have more formal mechanisms, such as committees or workshops established to purposefully scan for improvements and new technologies. Continually assessing new technologies and taking measures to develop and incorporate new technologies into the repository is a **best practice**.

All of the repositories request acknowledgment in publications if their resource is used in research, although few have actual requirements. At the academic-based and industry repositories, acknowledgment of the repository is requested but not required; at most of the government repositories, acknowledgment is contractually required and specific wording is suggested. Requiring acknowledgment of the repository, including specific language, is a **best practice** because it raises the visibility of the resource and may encourage future donations and use of the resource.

Best Practices for Privacy, Ethical Concerns, and Consent Issues

Some repositories keep identifiable information on tissue sources at the collection sites rather than at the main repository site. All of the repositories that keep identifiable information on site generally limit access to identifiable information to select staff. A few repositories use the "honest broker" model, which uses a neutral intermediary, between the individual whose tissue and data are being studied and the researcher, to collect and collate pertinent information regarding the tissue source, replace identifiers with a code, and release only coded information to the researcher. Limiting access to the codes that link patients' identifying information to their tissue specimens through physical and/or cyber procedures is a **best practice** to ensure that patient privacy and confidentiality are protected. (For details on best practices for privacy, ethical concerns, and consent issues practiced by each repository see Table 10.8.)

IRBs are responsible for the oversight and review of research that involves human participants to ensure that their privacy is protected and data confidentiality is maintained. All of the repositories evaluated use an IRB to oversee the repository practices, and most of them require researchers requesting samples to have IRB approval for their research. Some of the repositories also rely on separate bioethics advisory boards or committees to oversee privacy and confidentiality procedures. Requiring repositories to have IRB approval for the collection, storage, and distribution of biospecimens and associated data,

Table 10.8
Best Practices for Privacy, Ethical Concerns, and Consent Issues

Privacy, Ethical Concerns, and Consent Issues	CHTN	TARP	EDRN	Philadelphia Familial BCR	NHLBI/BBI	AFIP	Duke University Breast SPORE	Mayo Clinic Prostate SPORE	UAB Breast & Ovarian SPOREs	Univ. of Pittsburgh HSTB	Ardais	GCI
Limit access to codes that link patient identifying information to their tissue specimens through physical and/or cyber procedures	✔	✔	✔	✔	✔	✔	✔	✔	✔	✔	✔	✔
Use IRB oversight of repository practices	✔	✔	✔	✔	✔	✔	✔	✔	✔	✔	✔	✔
Require IRB review of research for researchers requesting samples	✔		✔	✔	✔	✔		✔	✔	✔	✔	✔
Use bioethics advisory board or other governance and oversight board/ committee to oversee privacy/confidentiality procedures	✔		✔	✔						✔	✔	✔
Obtain specimens obtained from fully consented tissue sources	✗	✗	✔	✔	✗		✔	✔	✔	✔	✔	✔
Use tiered consent process	✗			✔			✔	✔	✔	✔		✔

NOTE: ✔ = repository fully incorporates this best practice; ✗ = repository incorporates some aspects of this best practice.

and requiring researchers requesting samples to have IRB approval of the research projects that will use the samples are **best practices**. Having a bioethics advisory board or other governance and oversight board/committee to oversee privacy and confidentiality procedures is a **best practice** that provides another layer of review.

At all of the repositories evaluated where specific informed consent is obtained for the collection of biospecimens, it is obtained separately from the surgical consent. Some repositories use a tiered consent process that allows individuals to choose the type of specimen(s), if any, they want to donate (e.g., tissue, blood, or urine), the type of research for which the specimen(s) may be used (e.g., a specific research project, general research, or genetic research), and whether their medical records and outcomes data can be accessed and appended to the specimen for use in research. Obtaining biospecimens from individuals who are fully informed about and have consented to the collection of their tissue by the repository and its use for research purposes, and using a tiered consent process are **best practices**. Ideally, the consent process should occur separately from the surgical consent. However, since this is not always possible, at a minimum the informed consent for the collection and research use of specimens should be a separate section of the surgical consent form that requires a separate signature.

Best Practices for Intellectual Property and Legal Issues

Individuals who contribute biospecimens must have the right to withdraw their consent and have their tissue removed from the repository, a requirement for all federally funded research in the federal regulations governing research with human participants. However, in cases were the tissue has been stripped of identifiers and the link back to the tissue source has been destroyed, it is not possible to retrieve the tissue to withdraw it from the repository. Not only should the tissue be removed from the repository, but all data and computer records should be destroyed. Beyond the right to withdraw their tissue and data from the repository, tissue sources are given no other rights to their tissues by most repositories. It is a **best practice** to allow an individual who contributes tissue to a repository to withdraw consent and have the tissue, data, and computer records removed from the repository if the tissue retains identifiers to link it to that individual and it has not already been distributed to researchers. (For details on best practices for intellectual property and legal issues practiced by each repository see Table 10.9.)

Table 10.9
Best Practices for Intellectual Property and Legal Issues

Intellectual Property and Legal Issues	CHTN	TARP	EDRN	Philadelphia Familial BCR	NHLBI/BBI	AFIP	Duke University Breast SPORE	Mayo Clinic Prostate SPORE	UAB Breast & Ovarian SPOREs	Univ. of Pittsburgh HSTB	Ardais	GCI
Develop and adhere to specific IP policy		X		✔	X					✔		
Allow tissue sources to withdraw samples if they are not anonymized	✔			✔	✔ a	✔	✔	✔	✔	✔	✔	X
Use a formal agreement with researchers that specifies appropriate sample use	✔	✔ b		✔			✔		✔	✔	✔	✔
Specify responsibility for assuming risks for use of biospecimens in tissue use agreements	✔	✔ b		✔					✔	X	X	
Carefully review researcher submissions and credentials	✔	✔ b	✔	✔	✔ a	✔	✔	✔	✔	✔	X	X

NOTE: ✔ = repository fully incorporates this best practice; X = repository incorporates some aspects of this best practice.
a These best practices were specifically noted for NHLBI's LAM study.
b Requests for TARP microarrays are handled by CHTN Eastern Division.

The majority of repositories do not retain downstream rights to any intellectual property produced through the use of the tissue they distribute, with the exception of collaborative research, in which case the intellectual property rights are shared. The Cancer Family Registries sites do retain custody of and have primary rights to their data. Some repositories have no specific policies on intellectual policy for the distribution of biospecimens. To promote clarity, prevent potential legal confusion, and avoid conflicts with tissue sources, researchers using the tissue, and institutions contributing biospecimens, a

best practice is to use a specific published policy on intellectual property regarding research use of samples from the repository.

In most cases, institutions that contribute biospecimens to the repository give up their rights to the biospecimens as well. However, some contributing institutions are given priority for tissue requests. A **best practice** is to prioritize tissue distribution based on need while reserving a small percentage of tissue for contributing institutions participating in the repository.

Most of the repositories require researchers to sign some kind of agreement for the use of tissue that covers the legal issues associated with the use of biospecimens from their repositories. These tissue use agreements usually contain language to the effect that the researcher agrees that the specimens will be used only for the purposes cited in the application, no attempt to obtain identifying information will be made, no specimens will be sold or shared with a third party without the prior written permission of the repository, all specimens will be treated as potentially infectious, all personnel who will be handling the specimens will be properly trained, there is no implied warranty on the specimens; any publications resulting from the use of repository specimens will acknowledge the repository, and the researcher/institution using the tissue assumes responsibility for all risks associated with the receipt, handling, storage, and use of the tissue. The use of a tissue use agreement is a **best practice**.

None of the repositories have experienced liability issues regarding safety issues associated with the use of the specimens, loss of privacy or breach of confidentiality of tissue sources, claims by tissue sources of physical/psychosocial harms, or claims by tissue sources to property rights for discoveries made using their tissue. Even so, it is a **best practice** to explicitly specify the responsibility for assuming risks in connection with use of biospecimens in tissue use agreements, to fully inform tissue sources about risks to their rights and welfare, and to clarify ownership issues during the informed consent process. Similarly, it is a **best practice** to carefully review researcher submissions and credentials to ensure that tissue is being used by legitimate researchers for legitimate purposes. This review should include the inspection of IRB documentation, review of the study design for which the samples will be used, and verification that the researcher requesting samples is associated with a legitimate research institution.

Best Practices for Public Relations, Marketing, and Education
Public relations, marketing, and education are critical to the success of any tissue repository. The repositories evaluated use a combination of approaches to increase the visibility of their resource and mission, including exhibits at scientific meetings, advertising in scientific journals, newsletters, Web sites, direct mailings, and word of mouth. Some of the smaller repositories at universities do not market their resources at all. Using a combination of approaches to advertise the resources available at the repository is a **best practice**. (For details on best practices for public relations, marketing, and education practiced by each repository see Table 10.10.)

Few of the repositories have active education for and communications with tissue sources, such as sponsoring scientific and patient

Table 10.10
Best Practices for Public Relations, Marketing, and Education

Public Relations, Marketing, and Education	CHTN	TARP	EDRN	Philadelphia Familial BCR	NHLBI/BBI	AFIP	Duke University Breast SPORE	Mayo Clinic Prostate SPORE	UAB Breast & Ovarian SPOREs	Univ. of Pittsburgh HSTB	Ardais	GCI
Market the tissue resource, using word of mouth, journal ads, and exhibits at scientific meetings	✔	✔	✔			✔				✕	✔	✔
Provide information about generalized research findings to tissue sources, physicians, and researchers				✔	✕			✕		✕		✕

NOTE: ✔ = repository fully incorporates this best practice; ✕ = repository incorporates some aspects of this best practice.

workshops that report generalized research findings, disseminating research news and patient education information on a Web site, and sending newsletters to tissue sources and researchers summarizing research with repository resources. Although not widely done today, a **best practice** for repositories is to provide feedback to tissue sources and physicians about generalized findings from research with repository resources, through the Internet, sessions at scientific meetings, newsletters, or other outreach venues.

Conclusions

Each of the repositories evaluated in this study was designed according to a specific vision, which was not necessarily the same as the vision of the NBN Design Team. Due to these different visions, none of the repositories in this report exhibit *all* of the elements identified as important by the NBN Design Team for the proposed NBN. However, in most cases the repositories are flexible and, with appropriate funding and guidelines, have the potential to be an integral part of the NBN. In fact, this study revealed that most of the repositories have undergone a significant learning curve and that their current successes are based on years of experience and learning from early operations. This wealth of experience should not be overlooked as NDC goes forward with its plan to establish a new NBN.

All of the repositories exhibit some characteristics that would be useful for an NBN, but some of the repositories incorporate more of the NBN Design Team requirements than others do. CHTN, University of Pittsburgh HSTB, Ardais, and GCI have several of the characteristics identified by the NBN Design Team as necessary for a successful NBN. CHTN is a virtual network with the proven ability to distribute tens of thousands of biospecimens in a variety of forms (e.g., fresh, snap frozen, and paraffin embedded) to meet researchers' needs. University of Pittsburgh HSTB has developed a Web-based bioinformatics system that includes proteomics and genomics information and is already being used in Pennsylvania to create a virtual network of repositories. Ardais and GCI, the two private companies included in this study, have streamlined their specimen collection, processing, storage, and distribution through specific standard operating procedures, and they both minimize operator and data entry errors through the use of bar-code systems.

Other repositories have only a few of the key components of the proposed NBN. For example, TARP develops and disseminates tissue microarrays for high-throughput screening of multiple-tumor tissue (300 to 500 tissue specimens per array). EDRN requires that specimens be collected, processed, and annotated in a standardized manner and that a set of common data elements be collected with each specimen. Philadelphia Familial Breast Cancer Registry also uses common data elements and routinely collects longitudinal data. The SPOREs at Duke University, Mayo Clinic, and UAB routinely collect detailed clinical information and longitudinal data.

Whether NDC decides to build a brand new repository or to use existing repositories in the development of the NBN, learning from the existing repositories will be an important step. This report identifies the best practices at twelve biospecimen repositories in the United States. As the NBN gets under way, more detailed analyses of existing biospecimen repositories and the inclusion of key personnel from existing repositories will be warranted.

Interview Instrument for RAND Evaluation of Existing Tissue Resources

A. General

1. Can you give us some history/background about your repository?
2. What was the main purpose for developing the repository?
3. Do you belong to a professional organization that deals with specimen collection?

B. Biospecimen Collection, Processing, and Storage

Biospecimen Collection

The following questions cover your tissue collection techniques and standards:

1. Who are the sources of the tissue (e.g., patients, volunteers)? How were donors recruited?
2. Do you collect samples from minority populations? from the aged? from children? donors outside the United States?
   - Do the proportions of samples contained in your repository reflect the ethnic diversity in the general U.S. population?
3. Why were the tissue samples originally collected (e.g., diagnostic purposes, research)?
4. Who is responsible for collecting the samples for the repository (surgeons, pathologists, researchers, trained repository personnel)?

5. How many people do you employ to collect, store, process, and distribute tissue?

6. Where are the samples collected (e.g., community hospitals, academic medical centers)?

7. How do the samples get transferred to the repository? Or are they stored locally?

8. What kind of quality control, auditing, and/or standardization is performed during the collection of tissue?
   - How are these standards assured at the participating institutions that contribute tissue?
   - Are certain standards required of the institutions that agree to participate by contributing tissue? Are they dismissed if they do not adhere to these standards?

Biospecimen Storage

9. Can you share with us the storage techniques and standards you use for tissue in your repository?

10. How many and what types of tissue do you have in storage (for example, tissue from cancer patients, tissue from patients with rare diseases, etc.)? Is tissue collected from normal controls?

11. What types of tissue are collected, stored, available along with samples of diseased tissue (healthy adjacent tissue, blood, serum)?

12. How is tissue stored—in liquid nitrogen freezers, mechanical freezers, or both?
   - What maintenance and backup procedures do you have for the freezers?
   - What are your procedures/standards for storage of biospecimens in mechanical freezers (–80°C) and in liquid nitrogen?

13. In what form is tissue stored (e.g., fresh frozen, paraffin block)? For how long?

14. Do you attempt to keep your stock of tissue at a certain level, either numerically or as a distribution of various types of samples? If so, what techniques are used to maintain these levels (e.g., recruitment of additional medical facilities)?

15. What kind of quality control, auditing, and/or standardization is performed during the storage of tissue?

Biospecimen Processing and Annotation

16. Can you share with us the processing and annotation techniques and standards you use for tissue stored in your repository?
17. Is there a basic set of tests conducted on each sample to characterize the tissue (gene arrays, DNA/RNA studies, immunohistochemistry [histopathology], other)?
18. What kind of data are available about each sample (clinical, longitudinal, pathology report, diagnostic, demographic [gender, ethnicity], medical history, family history, genetic profile, environmental exposure, treatment outcomes data, recurrence, survival, etc.)?
19. If you collect longitudinal data, how are they tracked?
20. What kind of quality control, auditing, and/or standardization is performed during the processing and annotation of tissue?

C. Consumer/User Needs

1. Can you tell us about your tissue distribution policies?
   - How do you review and prioritize requests for tissue?
   - How do you prioritize the distribution of rare/precious tissue?
2. How many tissue samples do you distribute and to whom?
3. Who are your consumers/users? From what types of institutions are your consumers/users (academic, industry, government)? What is the relative proportion of types of users (e.g., 60% academic; 40% industry)?
4. Do researchers from certain institutions or researchers conducting certain types of research receive priority?
5. Are any of your samples distributed internationally?
6. For what purposes has the stored tissue been used (e.g., cancer research, gene mapping, genomics/proteomics)?
7. Do you believe there are unmet users' needs that are beyond your control to meet? If yes, what are they?
8. What kind of quality control, auditing, and/or standardization is performed during the distribution of tissue?

D. Bioinformatics and Data Management

The following questions concern your data storage, distribution, and analysis techniques and standards:

1. For what do you use your bioinformatics system (tracking of collection, processing, distribution and analysis of samples, histopathological data sets, clinical/outcomes information, results of research)?

2. Does your bioinformatics system contain any genomics/proteomics data?

3. What kind of quality control, auditing, and/or standardization is performed on data entered into your data repository/bioinformatics system? Standardized data reporting and data entry?

4. Is the data repository (bioinformatics system) aggregated? searchable? For example, can a researcher query the database to determine whether you have X numbers of samples for a particular disease?

5. Is your data repository set up so that automated extraction of information (data mining) is possible—i.e., is the data repository (bioinformatics system) "minable"? (NOTE: Data mining is part of a larger process called knowledge discovery; specifically, the step in which advanced statistical analysis and modeling techniques are applied to the data to find useful patterns and relationships.)

6. Does the extent of the access to the data in the repository differ for these different groups of people: physicians, researchers, employees, insurers, employers? If so, what are the differences?

7. Are any of the data from your repository about the tissue publicly available? Are they available on the World Wide Web? Who has access to the data (e.g., physicians, researchers, insurers, employers)?

8. Do any data from research performed on the tissue feed back into the repository data system (e.g., re-entry of relevant outcomes or research results)? If so, how do you validate the results that come back into the database?

9. What kinds of network security do you employ (encryption algorithms, firewalls, intrusion detection, etc.)?
10. How does the medical informatics system located at the collection site (i.e., hospital, laboratory) interface with the tissue bank's bioinformatics system?
11. Who develops your informatics systems? How many people do you employ in bioinformatics?

E. Business Plan and Operations

1. With whom or how were the arrangements made between the institutions that provide the tissue and the repositories? Was this arranged through the medical facility's administration or through individual doctors?
2. Can you share with us any lessons learned from setting up the medical institution/repository relationships? The donor/repository relationships?
3. Are you primarily involved in tissue banking, or do you collect tissue prospectively for distribution to particular researchers or for specific studies?
4. Is the tissue repository centralized, decentralized, or a centralized resource deployed through a virtual network of geographically dispersed tissue centers?
5. How is your repository funded—privately, publicly, some combination of the two?
6. How much does it cost your organization to collect, process, store, and distribute tissue? Per sample? Yearly?
7. How much does it cost a researcher to obtain tissue from your repository?
8. Do you regularly evaluate whether the resource is effectively used and, if so, how do you measure this?
9. What procedures are in place for improving specimen collection, storage, annotation, and distribution based on the development of new technologies? How do you plan for new technology?

10. Have you had to deal with any institutional barriers to collecting, storing, distributing, or using the tissue for research purposes? If so, how did you overcome them?

11. Can you share with us any "best practices" and standard operating procedures that are in place for your repository, including those that address sample and data handling, ethical, legal and social issues, and intellectual property issues?

12. Can you identify procedures within your existing operating structure that you would change? For example, if you were starting over, what would you do differently (e.g., eliminate procedures, add procedures, etc.)?

13. Do you have a reporting mechanism to track the use of your specimens including the number of specimens that are distributed each year?

14. Do researchers who use specimens from your repository cite/ acknowledge the use of repository specimens in a standardized manner?

F. Privacy, Ethical Concerns, and Consent Issues

Privacy Issues

1. What kind of personal/identifying information about the patient/donor is stored with the tissue? Is tissue in the repository:
   - unidentified—i.e., identifiable information was not collected or, if collected, not maintained and cannot be retrieved by the repository?
   - identified—i.e., the tissue is linked to personal information in such a way that the person from whom the material was obtained could be identified by name, patient number, or clear family relationship?

2. When tissue is distributed to researchers, what kind of personal information is sent with it? Are the samples given to the researchers:
   - unidentified samples—i.e., samples and data supplied by repositories to researchers from a collection of unidentified tissue (sometimes called "anonymous")?
   - unlinked samples—i.e., samples and data lack identifiers or codes that can link particular samples to an identified specimen or a particular human being (sometimes called "anonymized")?
   - coded samples—i.e., samples and data supplied by repositories to researchers from identified tissue with a code rather than with personally identifying information, such as a name or social security number (sometimes called "linked" or "identifiable")?
   - identified samples—i.e., samples and data supplied by repositories from identified tissue with a personal identifier (such as a name or patient number) that would allow the researcher to link the biological information derived from the research directly to the individual from whom the material was obtained?
3. What policies and procedures do you use to ensure that patient/donor privacy is protected? How do you ensure confidentiality of patient information?
4. How have repository processes changed as a result of the new HIPAA regulations?
5. What impact do state privacy laws have on your repository?

Consent Issues
6. What type of informed consent is obtained from each patient/donor (general consent for any type of research versus explicit/specific consent for an individual research project)?
7. Does consent for tissue donation occur with or separate from consent for the treatment/surgical procedure?
8. Do you use a consent interview? If so,
   - what type of individual conducts the interview?
   - for whom does this individual work (the hospital, the repository)?

9. Can you share with us a copy of your informed consent form, and policies and procedures?

Institutional Review Boards

10. Does your repository have an institutional review board (IRB) or have IRB approval (from whom)?
11. What kind of IRB approval is needed for researchers to use the samples?

G. Intellectual Property and Other Legal Issues

1. What kinds of policies do you have in place regarding intellectual property rights?
2. What rights does the submitting institution/researcher have to the tissue once it is given to the repository?
3. What rights do the individuals donating the tissue have once it is given to the repository?
4. Do they have access to their own tissue once it is donated (e.g., for medical purposes, for research purposes)?
5. Do you (the repository) retain any rights to the tissue once it has been transferred to the user?
   - Do researchers have to sign an agreement/contract to obtain samples?
   - Do you use a materials transfer agreement (MTA)? Can you share with us a copy of your materials transfer agreement?
6. Are donors compensated in any way for their tissue?
7. What kinds of policies are in place, if any, regarding publication review and approval, proper acknowledgment of the resource, and reporting of publications (e.g., to help the repository measure the impact of what has come out of the resource)?
8. How do you address liability issues associated with collection, distribution, and use of samples in your repository? Insurance, researchers sign a release?

9. Has there ever been an incident or legal action involving the collection, distribution, and/or use of samples in the repository and, if so, how was this resolved?
10. What kind of security do you use to ensure that the persons requesting tissue are legitimate?

H. Public Relations, Marketing and Education

1. How do you market your tissue resource to researchers (booths at scientific meetings, advertising in journals, word of mouth)?
2. What kind of post-research communications do you have with patients who donated their tissue, if any?
   • Future discoveries and therapeutic advances
   • Results of research with their samples—general results of research versus individual patient results
   • Patient education
   • Contributions to patient care
3. Do you release any information back to the donors of the tissue?

Glossary

Bioinformatics. Research, development, or application of computational tools and approaches for expanding the use of biological, medical, behavioral, or health data, including those to acquire, store, organize, archive, analyze, or visualize such data (as defined by the NIH Biomedical Information Science and Technology Initiative Consortium; http://www.bisti.nih.gov/CompuBioDef.pdf).

Biospecimen. Includes everything from subcellular structures such as DNA, to cells, tissue (bone, muscle, connective tissue, and skin), organs (e.g., liver, bladder, heart, kidney), blood, gametes (sperm and ova), embryos, fetal tissue, and waste (urine, feces, sweat, hair and nail clippings, shed epithelial cells, placenta).

Case. When a patient enters the hospital for a biopsy or surgery, the resulting tissue is accessioned in the pathology department as a single case.

Coded samples. Samples and data supplied by repositories to researchers from identified tissues with a code rather than with personally identifying information (such as a name or Social Security number). (Coded samples are sometimes called *linked* or *identifiable.*)

Data mining. Part of a larger process called *knowledge discovery;* specifically, the step in which advanced statistical analysis and modeling techniques are applied to the data to find useful patterns and relationships. Also, sorting through data to identify patterns and establish relationships.

De-identified protected health information. Health information that does not identify an individual and with respect to which there is no reasonable basis to believe that the information can be used to identify an individual. Such information is not individually identifiable health information (45 C.F.R. §164.514(a)-(c)).

Genomics. The study of genes and their function; the study of all or a substantial portion of the genes of an organism as a dynamic system, over time, to determine how those genes interact and influence biological pathways, networks, and physiology.

Honest broker. A neutral intermediary between the individual whose tissue and data are being studied and the researcher. The honest broker collects and collates pertinent information regarding the tissue source, replaces identifiers with a code, and releases only coded information to the researcher.

Identifiable. Tissue that is linked to personal information in such a way that the person from whom the material was obtained could be identified by name, patient number, or clear family relationship is considered identifiable.

Identified samples. Samples and data supplied by repositories from identified tissue with a personal identifier (such as a name or patient number) that would allow the researcher to link the biological information derived from the research directly to the individual from whom the material was obtained.

in silico. In or by means of a computer simulation; in a virtual environment, such as a computer simulation.

Matching adjacent tissue. Tissue collected during surgery that is next to the diseased tissue, but appears normal by virtual inspection under a microscope.

Minable. Data mining is part of a larger process called knowledge discovery; specifically, the step in which advanced statistical analysis and modeling techniques are applied to the data to find useful patterns and relationships.

Normal tissue. Non-diseased tissue from autopsy, organ donation, or patients undergoing surgery for a condition other than the one under study; usually used for a control in experiments with diseased tissue.

Parsing technique. A process of determining the structure of input; a technique to compare the input file against a standard content.

Discrepancies between the input and the standard are flagged as errors. In linguistics, parsing means dividing language into small components that can be analyzed. Parsing a sentence involves breaking it into words and phrases and identifying each component's type (e.g., verb, adjective, noun).

Patient. A person undergoing medical treatment.

Proteomics. The study of the full set of proteins encoded by a genome; the study of the identities, quantities, structures, and biochemical and cellular functions of all proteins in an organism, organ, or organelle, and how these properties vary in space, time, and physiological state.

Quality assurance. A program for the systematic monitoring and evaluation of the various aspects of a project, service, or facility to ensure that standards of quality are being met.

Quality control. Activities designed to ensure adequate quality; the process of assuring that certain desired characteristics of a product are being attained.

Sample. When portions of specimens are distributed to researchers, the researcher is receiving a *sample* of that specimen.

Searchable. A database that can be queried by a researcher to determine whether certain samples with certain characteristics are available is searchable.

Specimen. A portion of tissue, blood, or urine used for diagnosis and analysis. A single biopsy may generate several *specimens*, including a number of slides, paraffin blocks, and frozen specimens.

Tissue source. An individual from which a biospecimen is collected for research purposes. A tissue source may be an individual who has volunteered and has consented to participate in a clinical trial or other research project and to contribute tissue for research use, or an individual whose tissue that remains after medical treatment/ diagnosis or autopsy is used for research purposes for which consent has been waived.

Unidentifiable. Tissue for which identifiable information was not collected or, if collected, was not maintained and cannot be retrieved by the repository.

Unidentified samples. Samples and data supplied by repositories to researchers from a collection of unidentified tissue (sometimes called *anonymous*).

Unlinked samples. Samples and data that lack identifiers or codes that can link them to an identified specimen or a particular human being (also called *anonymized*).

Volunteer. A person who has volunteered to participate in a clinical trial or other research project.

References

Berman, J. J., M. E. Edgerton, and B. A. Friedman, "The Tissue Microarray Data Exchange Specification: A Community-Based, Open Source Tool for Sharing Tissue Microarray Data," *BMC Medical Informatics and Decision Making*, 2003 3:5 [available at http://www.biomedcentral.com/1472-6947/3/5 as of September 20, 2003].

Cancer Family Registries, *Access Policies and Procedures Manual*, 2002 [available at http://www.cfr.epi.uci.edu/nci/access_manual_05-29-02.htm as of August 31, 2003].

Committee on Germplasm Resources, Division of Biological Sciences, Assembly of Life Sciences, National Research Council, *Conservation of Germplasm Resources: An Imperative*, Washington, DC: National Academy of Sciences, 1978.

Eiseman, E., and S. B. Haga, *Handbook of Human Tissue Resources: A National Resource of Human Tissue Sample*, Santa Monica, CA: The RAND Corporation, MR-954-OSTP, 1999.

Holland, N. T., M. T. Smith, B. Eskenazi, and M. Bastaki, "Biological Sample Collection and Processing for Molecular Epidemiological Studies," *Mutation Research*, 543:217–234, 2003 [available at http://ehs.sph.berkeley.edu/superfund/publications/03_holland_1.pdf as of November 3, 2003].

Merz, J. F., P. Sankar, S. E. Taube, and V. Livolski, "Use of Human Tissues in Research: Clarifying Clinician and Researcher Roles and Information Flows," *Journal of Investigative Medicine*, 45(5):252–257, 1997.

National Bioethics Advisory Commission, *Research Involving Human Biological Materials: Ethical Issues and Policy Guidance*, Rockville, MD:

NBAC, August 1999 [available at http://www.georgetown.edu/research/nrcbl/nbac/pubs.html as of September 8, 2003].

Office for Human Research Protections, "Issues to Consider in the Research Use of Stored Data or Tissues," November 7, 1997 [available at http://ohrp.osophs.dhhs.gov/humansubjects/guidance/reposit.htm as of August 31, 2003].